CHILLIES

SOPHIE
DUPUIS-GAULIER

CHILLIES

RECIPES, PROFILES
& INSPIRATION

PHOTOGRAPHY
Emanuela Cino
STYLING
Sophie Dupuis-Gaulier

MITCHELL
BEAZLEY

INTRODUCTION

hilli pepper is the most widely used spice in the world. Chilli peppers have been consumed by humans for thousands of years. They grow in the form of a pod, which may be slender or bulbous, and are rich in vitamins A and C. A chilli pepper ranges in colour from green to red to orange depending on how ripe it is. The hollow inside contains a large number of seeds rich in capsaicin, the molecule responsible for the 'spicy' taste. The earliest evidence of chilli pepper use was found in a cave in Tehuacán, Mexico. However, it is believed to have originated in Brazil before spreading throughout South America, where it has been used as a condiment, a vegetable and even as a medicine.

When Christopher Columbus arrived in the Americas in 1492, he noticed that 'the natives eat chilli peppers as we would eat apples'. Following the colonization of the Americas, the chilli pepper was introduced to Europe, where it gradually replaced black pepper, which was a rare and expensive commodity.

While chilli pepper was one of the last spices discovered, it is now the most widely used for cooking across the world, particularly in hot countries, where it grows well.

Thanks to the Portuguese, who exported it to Asia, and to Ferdinand Magellan, who introduced it to Africa, its geographic expansion was very rapid. Today it can be found across five continents.

While it is a staple of South and Central American cuisines, chilli pepper is also prevalent in the cuisines of Asia, India and Africa. Americans are not far behind in their use of chilli-based hot sauces (consumption has apparently even exceeded that of the omnipresent ketchup).

The chilli pepper is the fruit of the *Capsicum* plant, a member of the nightshade family, which also includes tomatoes and potatoes.

The word 'capsicum' comes from the Greek *kapto*, which means to bite ('the pepper that bites back'). *Capsicum* has been crossed many times, creating multiple varieties. However, there are only five domesticated species, all with the same ancestor (the pequin chilli pepper).

• CAPSICUM ANNUUM

This is the most commonly cultivated species of chilli pepper in the world. It covers many varieties, including peppers with thick flesh, like sweet peppers, but also large peppers with thin skin, like poblanos, as well as the cayenne group and short peppers, like jalapeños.

• CAPSICUM FRUTESCENS

The most famous chilli pepper of this species is Tabasco®. Another variety is the malagueta chilli pepper, a Brazilian chilli pepper which is very difficult to find outside the country. The most common name given to chilli peppers of this variety is bird's eye chilli. This is because birds, who, like reptiles, are not sensitive to the capsaicin molecule, eat them and spread their seeds widely.

• CAPSICUM BACCATUM

This species is called *ají* in Latin America. It is believed to have originated in Bolivia or Peru and has been cultivated since 2500BCE.

• CAPSICUM CHINENSE

This species likes warm and humid climates and is native to the Amazon basin. It comprises at least 40 varieties, including the explosively hot habanero chilli pepper. *Capsicum chinense* is mostly cultivated east of the Andes. Over time, it spread to the Caribbean islands.

• CAPSICUM PUBESCENS

This is the only domesticated form that no longer exists in the wild. The species originated in Bolivia and is believed to have been domesticated as far back as 6000BCE. It was the most common chilli pepper among the Incas. It is cultivated today in the Andes and on the high plateaus of Central America. Commonly known as rocoto, it grows in regions with a very narrow temperature spectrum and can withstand light frosts.

A common characteristic of all these varieties of chilli peppers is the pronounced spicy taste, which varies in intensity due to the level of capsaicin present. Capsaicin is a molecular compound that irritates the epithelium (the tissue that lines the outer surfaces of many internal organs, the inner surfaces of body cavities and the inner surfaces of blood vessels). The characteristic action of capsaicin involves activating the heat receptors in the skin, causing a burning sensation even though there is no increase in temperature.

In 1912, Wilbur Scoville, an American pharmacologist, created a scale to assess the strength of each chilli pepper based on its capsaicin content. This scale, which takes his name, ranges from 0 to over 2,000,000 units. For ease of assessment, there is a simplified Scoville scale ranging from 0 to 10 (see page 12), where 0 means the pepper has no capsaicin (such as sweet peppers) and 10 means it has an explosive heat (like habanero).

Until 2006, the Red Savina habanero chilli pepper was listed as the hottest pepper in the world, exceeding 500,000 on the Scoville scale. In 2006, it was ousted by the Naga Jolokia chilli pepper, grown in the Assam region of India, which measures 1,000,000 on the Scoville scale. And since 2009, the American Carolina Reaper chilli pepper has been considered the hottest in the world, measuring between 1,500,000 and 2,200,000 on the Scoville scale.

Only mammals are sensitive to capsaicin. The capsaicin molecule is fat-soluble and this is why it is advised to consume a dairy product (drink milk or eat yogurt) to reduce the heat of a chilli pepper. Drinking water, on the contrary, will tend to fuel the fire. It is also advisable to wear disposable gloves when handling chilli peppers to avoid burning your fingers. Also, be careful not to rub your eyes when cooking chillies!

Like many spices, chilli pepper is excellent for your health. It is found in many traditional medicines, which credit it – among other benefits – with digestive properties because it makes people salivate, which helps to pre-digest food. It also has anti-inflammatory and slimming properties (because it accelerates the metabolism), as well as bactericidal properties, which limit intestinal infections.

When eating chilli peppers, be careful about the amount you use. Adjust the amount based on your tolerance of capsaicin. Generally, the recipes in this book are not overly hot, even those using hot chilli peppers like habanero or rocoto. If you follow the recommended cooking method, you will be able to appreciate the flavour of these chilli peppers without the heat overwhelming it.

It is not always easy to distinguish the different varieties available in shops. You will often find them labelled generically as 'chilli', making it difficult to know the strength. In that case, you will need to test them. Wear gloves to do this. Remove the stalk from the pepper and cut it in half lengthways. Remove the seeds and membranes, which will greatly reduce its strength, before tasting the pepper. Little by little, your body and palate will get used to the capsaicin and you will find you can remove fewer and fewer seeds.

Finally (if you need any further persuasion), eating chilli peppers releases endorphins, the feel-good hormones... That could be enough to get you hooked!

CONTENTS

SCOVILLE SCALE

Below is a summary table of the simplified Scoville scale, indicating the intensity of the chilli peppers and the nature of the mouth feel.

EXPLOSIVE	10	+ 100 000	Habanero
VOLCANIC	9	50 000–100 000	Thai bird's eye chilli pepper
TORRID	8	30 000–50 000	Chi-chien chilli pepper, bird's eye chilli pepper, rocoto, cayenne pepper
BURNING	7	15 000–30 000	Tabasco
FIERY	6	5 000–15 000	Takanotsume, ají amarillo
STRONG	5	2 500–5 000	Jalapeño, hot paprika, Calabrian chilli pepper
HOT	4	1 500–2 500	Padrón pepper, Espelette pepper, Aleppo chilli pepper
LIVELY	3	1 000–1 500	Poblano chilli pepper, cascabel, Cheongyang gochu
WARM	2	500–1 000	Peperoncino, Kashmiri mirch chilli pepper
MILD	1	100–500	Sweet paprika
NEUTRAL	0	1–100	Sweet pepper, Landes sweet pepper

ANATOMY OF A CHILLI PEPPER

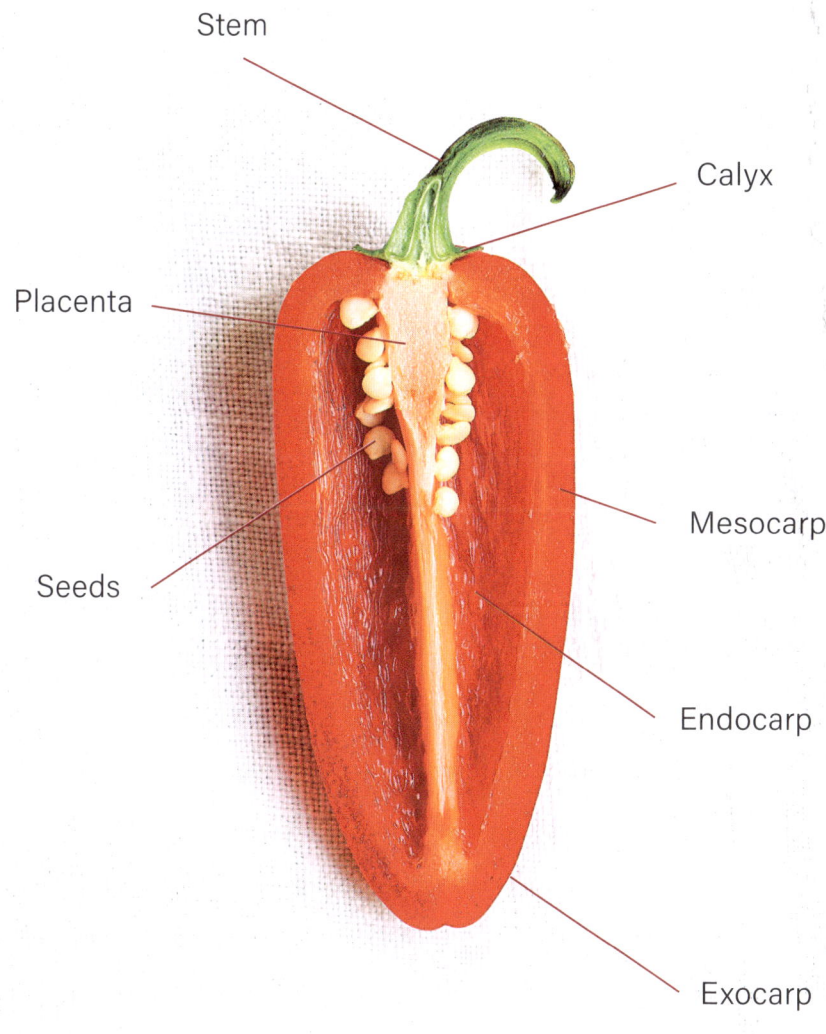

Stem

Calyx

Placenta

Seeds

Mesocarp

Endocarp

Exocarp

CHILLI PEPPER CATALOGUE

p. 16

SWEET PEPPER

p. 22

LANDES SWEET PEPPER

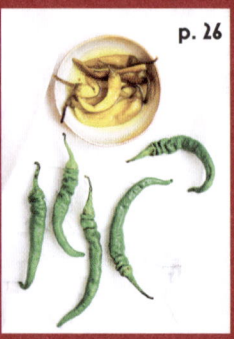
p. 26

PEPERONCINO

p. 32

KASHMIRI MIRCH CHILLI PEPPER

p. 38

POBLANO CHILLI PEPPER

p. 42

CASCABEL

p. 46

CHEONGYANG GOCHU

p. 54

PADRÓN PEPPER

p. 58

ESPELETTE PEPPER

p. 70

ALEPPO CHILLI PEPPER

p. 76

JALAPEÑO

p. 86

PAPRIKA

p. 96

CALABRIAN CHILLI PEPPER

p. 102

TAKANOTSUME

p. 106

AJÍ AMARILLO

p. 112

TABASCO®

p. 118

CHI-CHIEN CHILLI PEPPER

p. 124

BIRD'S EYE CHILLI PEPPER

p. 132

ROCOTO

p. 138

CAYENNE CHILLI PEPPER

p. 146

THAI BIRD'S EYE CHILLI PEPPER

p. 160

HABANERO

SWEET PEPPER

10	**SIZE** **10–18cm (4–7 inches) depending** **on the variety**
9	
	ORIGIN **Originally from Central America,**
8	**where Christopher Columbus** **encountered it, this appeared** **in Europe in the 16th century.**
7	
	WHERE IS IT EATEN? **It is found all over Europe.**
6	
	EATING **Found in the cuisine of many**
5	**countries, sweet pepper can be** **eaten raw and cooked. It is full** **of fibre and, when grilled or** **roasted, the skin can be peeled**
4	**away to make it easier to digest.** **The green pepper, which is still** **immature, is firmer and has a**
3	**slight bitterness; it is often found** **in ratatouilles. The red and yellow** **peppers, with a milder flavour,**
2	**are often used in coulis, sautéed,** **grilled or stuffed. Cut them into** **small raw cubes to add colour**
1	**and freshness to your salads.**
	PLANT
▶ 0	**Sweet pepper, or simply 'pepper'** **in Europe, is the common name** **of *Capsicum annuum*.**

The sweet pepper belongs to the nightshade family (just like potatoes and tomatoes).

Its Scoville rating is zero because it contains no capsaicin (the active molecule in chilli peppers).

Its colour ranges from green to red or from green to orange or yellow: the colour changes as the pepper ripens. It can be conical in shape or square with lobes. All types are hollow and contain seeds and membranes which must be removed before cooking. The peak season is from June to September.

Sweet peppers are rich in vitamin C and antioxidants (carotenoids, flavonoids), which are present in increasing quantities as the pepper ripens.

They also have a natural diuretic role due to a high potassium level and low sodium content.

MARINATED SWEET PEPPERS

WITH GARLIC AND OLIVE OIL

𝓮 𝓮 𝓮 𝓮

PREPARATION: 15 MINS / COOKING: 30 MINS

SERVES 4–6

- 2 large yellow sweet peppers - 2 large red sweet peppers - 1 large garlic clove
- 5 tablespoons olive oil - 3 thyme sprigs - Salt and freshly ground black pepper

---

Baking tray - Nonstick baking paper - Freezer bag

1/ The day before you want to eat the dish, preheat the oven to 200°C fan (425°F) Gas Mark 7. Wash and dry the peppers. Place them on a baking tray lined with nonstick baking paper.

2/ Roast for 30 minutes, turning them over roughly every 8 minutes to ensure they do not burn (the skin should, however, become a little blackened).

3/ Take the sweet peppers out of the oven, put them in a freezer bag and let them cool.

4/ Remove the peppers from the bag. Remove the stem, skin and seeds. Cut the flesh into strips about 2cm (¾ inch) thick or leave the lobes whole. Arrange them on a serving dish.

5/ Peel the garlic clove and chop it finely. Spread the garlic and oil over the peppers. Strip the leaves from the thyme sprigs and sprinkle them over the peppers. Season with salt and pepper.

6/ Cover the dish and refrigerate overnight.

| EXTRA STRONG |

| STRONG |

| MEDIUM |

▶ | MILD

TIPS
Serve hot or cold with homemade croutons. If using spicy chorizo, combine with a mild (sweet) paprika. Use smoked paprika with mild chorizo.

CREAMED SWEET PEPPERS

WITH CHORIZO

ℓℓℓℓ

PREPARATION: 15 MINS / COOKING: 35 MINS

SERVES 4

• 450g (1lb) red sweet peppers • 1 garlic clove • 1 onion • 80g (2¾oz) mild or spicy chorizo (see Tips, page 20) • 3 tablespoons olive oil • 227g (8oz) can of chopped tomatoes with juice • 1 teaspoon dried oregano (plus extra to garnish) • ½ teaspoon smoked or sweet paprika (see Tips, page 20) • 300ml (½ pint) water • 1 tablespoon caster sugar • Salt

Heavy-based casserole pot • Blender • Sieve

1/ Wash and dry the peppers. Remove the stalks, seeds and white membranes. Cut the flesh into large pieces.

2/ Peel the garlic clove. Finely chop the garlic and onion.

3/ Remove the skin from the chorizo and cut it into small pieces.

4/ Heat the oil in a heavy-based casserole pot. Add the chopped onion and garlic. Allow them to brown for 5 minutes, stirring regularly. Add the sweet peppers, the tomatoes and their juice, the oregano, paprika and chorizo. Pour in the measured water. Add the sugar and season with salt. Cover and simmer for 30 minutes.

5/ Transfer everything to a blender and blend until smooth.

6/ Pass the blended liquid through a sieve to remove any remaining pepper skin.

7/ Serve the soup garnished with a sprinkle of dried oregano.

EXTRA STRONG | STRONG | MEDIUM | MILD

LANDES SWEET PEPPER

10

SIZE
15cm (6 inches)

9

ORIGIN
It is originally from the Landes
region of France.

8

WHERE IS IT EATEN?
It is mainly consumed locally
in the Basque Country in Spain.

7

6

EATING
It is often used in recipes
for piperade. It can be eaten
stuffed and fried, or raw in
salads. It can also be served
as a jam to accompany sweet
and sour dishes.

5

4

PLANT
The Landes sweet pepper
belongs, like other peppers,
to the nightshade family,
specifically to the species
Capsicum annuum.

3

2

1

▶ **0**

This is a very sweet pepper.

Its Scoville rating is zero because it contains no
capsaicin (the active molecule in chilli peppers).

The Landes sweet pepper is a long, thin
pepper. For cultivation, it requires an oceanic
climate: hot and humid. It is harvested from
July to the end of November, with harvesting
ending at the first frost.

Its shape (straight or curved) depends on
climatic conditions. A long, straight pepper is
one that has grown well and has not suffered
from adverse weather conditions.

It is green or red in colour. Immature green
peppers have thicker skin and a slight
bitterness, while the red peppers, picked
when fully ripe, have thinner skin and a
sweeter flavour.

PIPERADE

ɾɾɾɾ

PREPARATION: 25 MINS / COOKING: 40 MINS

SERVES 4

▪ 500g (1lb 2oz) Landes sweet peppers ▪ 500g (1lb 2oz) tomatoes ▪ 2 garlic cloves
▪ 300g (10½oz) onions ▪ 4 thyme sprigs ▪ 5 tablespoons olive oil ▪ 2 tablespoons caster
sugar (adjust depending on the ripeness of the tomatoes) ▪ 2 tablespoons tomato purée
▪ 1 thick slice Bayonne ham (or other dry-cured ham, such as prosciutto)
▪ 2 eggs, beaten (optional) ▪ Salt

1/ Wash and dry the sweet peppers. Remove the stems and cut them in half lengthways. Remove the seeds and cut into sections of about 1cm (½ inch).

2/ Place the tomatoes in a bowl and pour over boiling water to cover. Leave for 1–2 minutes, then drain, cut a cross at the stem end of each tomato, and peel off the skins. Cut them into quarters and remove the seeds.

3/ Peel the garlic cloves. Finely chop the garlic and onions. Strip the leaves from the thyme sprigs.

4/ Heat the olive oil in a deep frying pan. Add the chopped onions and garlic and let them soften over low heat for 5 minutes. Add the peppers. After 15 minutes, add the tomatoes, sugar, tomato purée and thyme leaves. Season with salt and simmer for 20 minutes.

5/ Cut the Bayonne ham into strips and brown them in a dry frying pan.

6/ Transfer the piperade to a serving dish and top with the Bayonne ham.

7/ If you wish, make an omelette using the 2 beaten eggs to serve alongside.

EXTRA STRONG | STRONG | MEDIUM | ▶ MILD

PEPERONCINO

10
—
9
—
8
—
7
—
6
—
5
—
4
—
3
·
▶ **2**
—
1
—

0
—

SIZE
5-7cm (2-2¾ inches)

ORIGIN
This pepper is native to Puglia, in Italy.

WHERE IS IT EATEN?
It is a classic ingredient in Italian gastronomy. It is also found in Greece.

EATING
Peperoncini are often pickled in brine and can be used in place of gherkins in sandwiches. They are also eaten raw cut into slices and can be found in antipasti, on pizzas and in salads.

PLANT
The plants fruit heavily and often require stakes.

The peperoncino chilli pepper belongs to the nightshade family, specifically to the species *Capsicum annuum*.

It is a relatively mild chilli pepper.

It is rated 1–2 on the simplified Scoville scale.

The peperoncino is also known as *friggitello*, *peperone*, Tuscan pepper or golden Greek pepper.

It needs a warm, sunny climate to grow.

When fresh and unpickled, the fruits are green.

TIP
You can add a little chilli oil on top of the pizza just before serving (see page 101).

PIZZA WITH MARINATED VEGETABLES
AND PEPERONCINO PEPPER

ϵϵϵϵ

PREPARATION: 20 MINS / MARINATING: 2 HOURS
RESTING (DOUGH): 2½ HOURS / COOKING: 35–40 MINS

FOR 1 PIZZA

FOR THE MARINATED VEGETABLES ▪ 2 garlic cloves ▪ ½ red onion ▪ 1 green courgette
▪ 1 small yellow courgette ▪ ¼ aubergine ▪ ½ red sweet pepper ▪ 1 teaspoon dried oregano
▪ 100ml (3½fl oz) olive oil **FOR THE DOUGH** ▪ 10g (¼oz) fresh yeast ▪ 200ml (⅓ pint) water
▪ 400g (14oz) 00 flour ▪ 10g (¼oz) salt ▪ 3 tablespoons olive oil (plus a little for the bowl)
FOR THE TOMATO SAUCE ▪ 1 garlic clove ▪ 1 tablespoon olive oil ▪ 200ml (⅓ pint) passata
▪ ½ teaspoon caster sugar ▪ 1 pinch of paprika ▪ 1 teaspoon dried oregano ▪ Salt and freshly
ground black pepper **FOR THE TOPPING** ▪ 6 cherry tomatoes ▪ 200g (7oz) mozzarella cheese
▪ 1 teaspoon dried oregano ▪ 4–6 peperoncino chilli peppers

**Garlic press ▪ Food processor with dough hook ▪ Rolling pin
▪ Baking tray ▪ Nonstick baking paper**

1/ PREPARE THE MARINATED VEGETABLES. Peel the garlic cloves. Crush the garlic using a garlic press and finely chop the onion. Wash and dry the vegetables. Cut the green courgette into thin tagliatelle-like strips using a peeler. Cut the other vegetables into slices ½cm (¼ inch) thick. Place all the vegetables in a large bowl. Add the garlic, oregano, olive oil and seasoning. Mix well and leave to marinate for at least 2 hours in a cool place.

2/ MEANWHILE, MAKE THE DOUGH. Crumble the yeast into a large bowl. Add 100ml (3½fl oz) of the measured water and 40g (1½oz) of the flour. Mix well and set aside for 30 minutes.

3/ Place the dough in the bowl of the food processor, add the rest of the flour, the salt, the olive oil and the remaining 100ml (3½fl oz) of water. Mix well, then knead for 10–12 minutes, until a ball of dough forms. Remove the dough from the bowl of the food processor and oil the bowl. Place the dough back in the bowl, cover it with a cloth and leave to rise for 2 hours.

4/ PREPARE THE TOMATO SAUCE. Peel the garlic clove and crush it using a garlic press. In a large, deep frying pan, heat the olive oil, add the garlic and cook gently for 3 minutes. Add the passata, sugar, paprika and oregano, season and simmer for 15 minutes.

5/ Preheat the oven to 230°C fan (485°F), Gas Mark 9½. Halve the tomatoes. Roll out the pizza dough and transfer to a baking tray lined with nonstick baking paper. Spread the tomato sauce over the dough, leaving a 2cm (¾ inch) margin. Distribute the mozzarella, marinated vegetables and cherry tomatoes on top. Sprinkle with oregano and bake for 15–20 minutes.

6/ Spread the peperoncino peppers on the pizza and serve immediately.

| EXTRA STRONG |
| STRONG |
| MEDIUM |
| MILD |

TIP
This recipe is relatively simple. Its success relies on the quality of the products used. You can easily find Cretan barley bread rusks at Greek delicatessens or online.

DAKOS SALAD

₡ ₡ ₡ ₡

PREPARATION: 15 MINS / RESTING: 15 MINS

SERVES 4

- 4 tomatoes ▪ ½ cucumber ▪ 6 peperoncino chilli peppers or golden Greek peppers
▪ ½ red onion ▪ 120g (4½oz) feta cheese ▪ 4 barley bread rusks ▪ 12 Kalamata olives,
pitted ▪ 1 tablespoon dried oregano ▪ 8 tablespoons olive oil
▪ Salt and freshly ground black pepper

1/ Wash and dry the tomatoes and cucumber. Remove the stems from the tomatoes
and cut them into quarters. Remove the seeds and cut each quarter in half.

2/ Cut the peperoncini into slices ½cm (¼ inch) thick. Cut the cucumber into sticks,
taking care to remove the seeds. Finely chop the onion. Cut the feta into small cubes.
Roughly crumble the barley bread rusks.

3/ Mix the tomatoes, cucumber, olives, oregano, feta, red onion, peperoncino slices and
barley bread rusks in a bowl. Drizzle with olive oil. Adjust the seasoning and let the
bread soak up the juices for about 15 minutes.

4/ Serve chilled.

| EXTRA STRONG |

| STRONG |

| MEDIUM |

▶ | MILD |

KASHMIRI MIRCH CHILLI PEPPER

10

9

8

7

6

5

4

3

▶ 2

1

0

SIZE
3–4cm (1¼–1½ inches)

ORIGIN
This pepper is originally from Kashmir (a region located between India, Pakistan and China).

WHERE IS IT EATEN?
It is found mainly in India.

EATING
This chilli pepper is mainly consumed in ground form. It has to be roasted before being blended into a fine powder. It should be stored away from air, humidity and light. Kashmiri mirch chilli pepper is also called *deghi* or *deggi mirch*. It is the flagship spice of rogan josh or butter chicken. It also pairs very well with eggs, vegetables (like sweet potato) and fish.

PLANT
Kashmiri mirch chilli pepper belongs to the nightshade family, specifically to the species *Capsicum annuum*.

This pepper is rated 2 on the simplified Scoville scale, similar to paprika.

Kashmiri mirch is a mild and fragrant chilli pepper, slightly sweet, and is often described as warm.

It is a very pronounced red colour, giving a suggestion of warmth and depth to dishes, which stimulates the taste buds. This is the chilli pepper used in the composition of tandoori spices.

This is a fairly rare and expensive chilli pepper, mostly used during festive meals. Its scarcity has led to a parallel market where it is often replaced by a hotter and cheaper chilli pepper.

TIPS

Serve with your favourite Indian breads like paratha, naan or chapati. The dough can be kept for 15 days in the refrigerator in an airtight container. There are ready-made curry pastes available commercially if you would prefer not to make the paste yourself.

LAMB ROGAN JOSH

CURRY

℮℮℮℮

PREPARATION: 45 MINS / MARINATING: 12 HOURS / COOKING: 1¾ HOURS

SERVES 4–6

FOR THE CURRY ▪ 3cm (1¼ inch) piece of fresh root ginger ▪ 6 garlic cloves
▪ 125g (4½oz) natural yogurt ▪ 1 teaspoon freshly ground black pepper ▪ 1 teaspoon ground turmeric ▪ 800g (1lb 12oz) lamb shoulder cut into large cubes **FOR THE CURRY PASTE**
▪ 1 red sweet pepper ▪ 3 small red onions ▪ 5 green cardamom pods ▪ 4 cloves ▪ 1 teaspoon coriander seeds ▪ 1 teaspoon cumin seeds ▪ 1 teaspoon fennel seeds ▪ 1 tablespoon ground cinnamon ▪ 3 dried Kashmiri mirch chillies or 1 teaspoon Kashmiri mirch chilli powder ▪ 3 tablespoons neutral vegetable oil (such as rapeseed, grapeseed or sunflower)
▪ 2 tablespoons paprika ▪ 500g (1lb 2oz) chopped tomatoes ▪ Salt
TO SERVE ▪ 3 mint sprigs

Pestle and mortar or blender

1/ **THE DAY BEFORE YOU WANT TO EAT THE DISH, PREPARE THE CURRY.** Peel the ginger and garlic cloves. Blend them together into a paste.

2/ In a large bowl, mix the yogurt, ground pepper, turmeric, and ginger and garlic paste. Add the pieces of lamb, mix well, cover and leave to marinate overnight in the refrigerator.

3/ **ON THE DAY OF SERVING, PREPARE THE CURRY PASTE.** Wash the sweet pepper. Cut it in half and remove the stalk, white membranes and seeds. Use a blender to blend the onions and sweet pepper together. Split open the cardamom pods and extract the small seeds to use.

4/ In a very hot frying pan, toast the cardamom seeds, cloves, coriander seeds, cumin seeds, fennel seeds and ground cinnamon. Using a pestle and mortar or a blender, crush together the pan-roasted seeds and the Kashmiri mirch.

5/ In the same frying pan that you used to toast the seeds, heat the oil, add the toasted and ground spices, the paprika and the onion mixture. Cook for 8–10 minutes, stirring constantly to prevent the paste from burning. Add the chopped tomatoes and 200ml (⅓ pint) of water. Add salt to taste. Mix well and cook for 5 minutes.

6/ Remove the lamb from the marinade. Pour the curry paste into a large, deep frying pan with a lid and add the lamb. Cover and cook over a medium heat for 1 hour. Remove the lid and allow to reduce for about 30 minutes.

7/ Sprinkle with chopped mint leaves just before serving.

EXTRA STRONG | STRONG | MEDIUM | MILD

TANDOORI

CHICKEN

ϵϵϵϵ

PREPARATION: 15 MINS / MARINATING: 3 HOURS / COOKING: 25-30 MINS

SERVES 4

4 chicken thighs ▪ 2 garlic cloves ▪ 4cm (1½ inch) piece of fresh root ginger ▪ 1 lime ▪ 200g (7oz) creamy natural yogurt ▪ ¼ teaspoon Kashmiri mirch chilli powder ▪ ¼ tablespoon ground cumin ▪ ¼ tablespoon ground coriander ▪ ½ teaspoon ground turmeric ▪ ¼ teaspoon ground cinnamon ▪ ¼ teaspoon freshly ground black pepper ▪ 1 teaspoon salt ▪ 1 tablespoon sunflower oil

---

Garlic press ▪ Grater ▪ Ovenproof dish

1/ Slash the chicken thighs with a knife. Peel the garlic cloves and ginger. Crush the garlic and grate the ginger. Squeeze the lime.

2/ In a large bowl, mix the yogurt with the lime juice, garlic, ginger, spices, black pepper, salt and oil.

3/ Place the chicken thighs in this marinade and mix well. Cover and refrigerate for 3 hours.

4/ Preheat the oven to 210°C fan (450°F), Gas Mark 8. Place the chicken in an ovenproof dish and bake for approximately 25–30 minutes, making sure to turn it over halfway through cooking.

EXTRA STRONG

STRONG

MEDIUM

MILD

SERVING SUGGESTION
Serve with a yogurt and coriander sauce.

BUTTER
CHICKEN

ℓℓℓℓ

PREPARATION: 25 MINS / MARINATING: 2 HOURS / COOKING: 40 MINS

SERVES 4

- 500g (1lb 2oz) chicken breast - 40g (1½oz) raw cashew nuts - 100ml (3½fl oz) double cream **FOR THE MARINADE** - 1 garlic clove - 2cm (¾ inch) piece of fresh root ginger - 125g (4½oz) thick natural yogurt - ½ teaspoon Kashmiri mirch chilli powder - 2 tablespoons ground almonds - ½ teaspoon sweet paprika - ¼ teaspoon ground cinnamon - 2 tablespoons sunflower oil **FOR THE BUTTER SAUCE** - 1 garlic clove - 1cm (½ inch) piece of fresh root ginger - 3 cardamom pods - 1 onion - 1 fresh green chilli pepper (Thai bird's eye chilli type) - 40g (1½oz) butter - 1 teaspoon ground coriander - 1 teaspoon ground fenugreek - 140g (5oz) tomato purée - 100ml (3½fl oz) passata - 2 tablespoons clear honey - 150ml (¼ pint) water **TO SERVE** - 4 fresh coriander sprigs - 1 lime

Garlic press - Grater - Baking tray - Nonstick baking paper

1/ **PREPARE THE MARINADE.** Peel the garlic clove and ginger. Crush the garlic and finely grate the ginger. In a large bowl, mix the yogurt, Kashmiri mirch chilli powder, garlic, ginger, ground almonds, paprika, cinnamon and oil.

2/ Cut the chicken into strips and add to the bowl with the marinade. Mix well, cover and refrigerate for 2 hours.

3/ Preheat the oven to 200°C fan (425°F), Gas Mark 7. Roughly drain the chicken and place it on a baking tray lined with nonstick baking paper. Bake for 15 minutes, making sure to turn it over halfway through cooking.

4/ **PREPARE THE SAUCE.** Peel the garlic clove and ginger. Crush the garlic and finely grate the ginger. Split open the cardamom pods. Finely chop the onion. Remove the stem of the fresh chilli pepper, discard the seeds and chop the flesh.

5/ In a hot frying pan, toast the cashew nuts.

6/ Melt the butter in a large, deep frying pan. Add the garlic, ginger, cardamom pods, chopped chilli pepper and onion and fry for about 10 minutes, stirring regularly. Add the ground coriander, fenugreek, tomato purée, passata, honey and the measured water. Mix well and simmer for 15 minutes.

7/ Add the chicken, cream and toasted cashew nuts.

8/ Serve with lime wedges and chopped coriander.

| EXTRA STRONG |

| STRONG |

| MEDIUM |

▶ | MILD |

POBLANO CHILLI PEPPER

DRIED VERSION: ANCHO

10

—

9

—

8

—

7

—

6

—

5

—

4

—

▶ 3

—

2

—

1

—

0

—

SIZE
15cm (6 inches) long and 8cm
(3¼ inches) wide

ORIGIN
It is originally from the state
of Puebla in Mexico.

WHERE IS IT EATEN?
It is very popular from South
America to the United States.

EATING
When fresh, it is used in the
typical dish enjoyed during
the Mexican national holiday:
chile relleno en nogada. It can
also be used in soups. Once dried,
it is used in the famous *mole
poblano* or in cocktails where it
is infused with alcohol (Smoky
Ancho Reyes).

PLANT
The ancho/poblano pepper
belongs to the nightshade family
and more specifically to the
species *Capsicum annuum*.

It has a low capsaicin content, which is
why it is classified as a mild pepper.

It ranks 2–3 on the simplified Scoville scale.

When fresh, the pepper is called a poblano
pepper or *chile poblano* (from the state
of Puebla).

It is a very fragrant pepper with notes of fresh
tobacco, chocolate and coffee.

It turns from green to dark red, or even almost
black, when fully ripe.

Once dried, it is called an ancho pepper, which
means large pepper: when dried, it loses its
length but retains its width.

SUBSTITUTIONS
You can substitute soured cream for the crème fraîche and replace yellow corn with white corn if you can find it.

CREAMED POBLANO

CHILLI PEPPER

ℓℓℓℓ

PREPARATION: 15 MINS / COOKING: 25 MINS

SERVES 4

• 2 garlic cloves • 2 onions • 8 poblano chilli peppers • 6 tablespoons neutral oil
(such as sunflower) • 1.2 litres (2 pints) vegetable or chicken stock • 4 tablespoons plain
flour • 80g (2¾oz) crème fraîche • 4 corn tortillas • 8 tablespoons canned sweetcorn • Salt

---

Heavy-based casserole pot • Blender

1/ Peel the garlic cloves. Finely chop the garlic and onions. Wash and dry the chilli
peppers. Remove the stalks, seeds and membranes and cut the flesh into large pieces.

2/ In a heavy-based casserole pot, heat the oil, add the chopped onions and leave
to brown for a few minutes. Add the garlic and chillies and continue cooking for
3 minutes. Pour in the vegetable stock and flour. Add salt, cover and cook for
20 minutes.

3/ Thoroughly blend the contents of the casserole pot with the crème fraîche, adjusting
the quantity of liquid depending on the desired consistency. Check the seasoning.

4/ Toast the tortillas in a dry frying pan. When they are crispy, cut them into pieces.

5/ Pour the soup into bowls and sprinkle with the sweetcorn and tortilla pieces.
Serve immediately.

EXTRA STRONG

STRONG

MEDIUM

▶ MILD

CASCABEL

SIZE
2–4cm (¾–1½ inches)

ORIGIN
This pepper is from Mexico (specifically the provinces of Coahuila, Durango, Guerrero and Jalisco).

WHERE IS IT EATEN?
It is found mainly in Mexico.

EATING
It is commonly used in sauces and stews.

PLANT
The cascabel chilli pepper belongs to the nightshade family, specifically to the species *Capsicum annuum*.

This chilli is rated 3 on the simplified Scoville scale.

The cascabel, also known as *chile bola*, is a round chilli pepper. When it is dried, its skin becomes very tough and the seeds rattle inside, making a sound like a rattlesnake.

Cascabel chilli peppers need to be soaked for a long time before use and should be chopped finely.

Cascabel chilli peppers give sauces an intense red colour, and the flesh provides a flavour rich in tannins. They have a woody and smoky taste, with notes of hazelnut and tobacco. Each chilli pepper weighs about 3–5g (⅒–⅛oz).

WARM LENTIL SALAD

WITH CASCABEL CHILLI PEPPER

ℓℓℓℓ

PREPARATION: 20 MINS / SOAKING: 12 HOURS (OPTIONAL) / COOKING: 55 MINS

SERVES 4

▪ 240g (9oz) green or brown lentils, dried ▪ 1 medium cascabel chilli pepper
▪ 2 garlic cloves ▪ 2 onions ▪ 150g (5½oz) button mushrooms ▪ 4 thyme sprigs
▪ 2 pinches of coarse salt ▪ 4 tablespoons olive oil

Pestle and mortar

1/ The day before you want to eat the dish, soak the lentils for 12 hours.

2/ On the day of serving, soak the chilli pepper in lukewarm water. Drain and rinse the lentils. Cover with water and simmer in a medium saucepan for 30–35 minutes, then drain and keep them warm.

3/ Peel the garlic cloves. Finely chop the garlic and onions. Remove the woody stem from the mushrooms and cut them into thin slices. Remove the stem and seeds from the chilli pepper. Strip the leaves from the thyme sprigs.

4/ Using a pestle and mortar, crush together the chilli pepper, thyme leaves, garlic cloves and coarse salt.

5/ Heat the oil in a frying pan, add the onions and sweat them by cooking over low heat for 10 minutes. Increase the heat and add the mushrooms and chilli paste. Continue cooking for 10 minutes. Add the lentils, mix well and adjust the seasoning.

| EXTRA STRONG |

► | STRONG |

| MEDIUM |

| MILD |

—

CHEONGYANG GOCHU

10 —

SIZE
4–5cm (1½–2 inches)

9 —

ORIGIN
This pepper is originally
from Korea.

8 —

WHERE IS IT EATEN?
It is found mainly in Korea
but can be sourced in Asian
grocery shops.

7 —

6 —

EATING
There are two types of ground
cheongyang gochu:
- finely ground gochugaru
  which is used in gochujang
  (chilli paste) and also in the
  recipe for radish water kimchi.
- gochugaru flakes found in
  kimchi recipes, spicy soups,
  stews, bibimbap, and so on.

5 —

4 —

▶ 3

PLANT
The Cheongyang gochu
chilli pepper belongs to the
nightshade family, specifically to
the species *Capsicum annuum*.

2 —

1 —

0 —

This is a chilli pepper with sweet, spicy and
slightly smoky flavours.

Cheongyang gochu is rated 3 on the simplified
Scoville scale.

As well as providing flavour, the ground
chilli pepper can also be used as an intense
colouring agent.

Koreans often make their own gochugaru
(*gochu* means 'chilli pepper' and *garu* means
'powder'). They buy their own dried chillies
from market stalls, remove the stalks and seeds,
and take them to a workshop where they can
be ground to varying levels of fineness.

Cheongyang gochu can be replaced in certain
recipes by Espelette pepper (see page 58).

KIMCHI

ɾɾɾɾ

PREPARATION: 30 MINS / RESTING (BRINING): 12 HOURS / FERMENTATION: 5 DAYS

MAKES 1 JAR OF APPROXIMATELY 900G (2LB)

▪ 1 Chinese cabbage, about 1.1kg (2lb 4oz) ▪ 160g (5¾oz) coarse salt ▪ 150g (5½oz) daikon (white radish) ▪ 3 large garlic cloves ▪ 20g (¾oz) fresh root ginger ▪ 30g (1oz) spring onions with green stems ▪ 1 small leek ▪ 30g (1oz) gochugaru chilli powder ▪ 2 tablespoons fish sauce (nam pla) ▪ 3 teaspoons caster sugar

Large airtight container ▪ Garlic press ▪ Grater ▪ Large airtight, sterilized jar

1/ The day before you make the kimchi you need to brine the cabbage. Remove any damaged cabbage leaves if necessary. Cut off the hard stem base. Cut the cabbage into thirds lengthways. Fill a large container with 1 litre (1¾ pints) of warm water and add 30g (1oz) coarse salt. Spread the remaining salt between the cabbage leaves. Place the salted cabbage in the container of water. Cover tightly and let the cabbage brine for 12 hours. Turn the cabbage over after 6 hours.

2/ On the following day, peel the daikon, garlic and ginger.

3/ Crush the garlic cloves in a garlic press, grate the ginger, finely chop the leek, cut the daikon into thin sticks and chop the spring onions (bulbs and stems).

4/ Mix the chilli powder, fish sauce and sugar in a bowl. Add the ginger, garlic, leek and daikon. Mix well.

5/ Rinse the cabbage under cold water and drain it. Cut it into smaller pieces if you wish. Spread the paste well between the cabbage leaves, then place the cabbage in a large airtight jar.

6/ Pack well so that there is no air between the cabbage leaves. Seal and leave at room temperature for 2 days, then refrigerate for 3 days.

7/ Kimchi can be stored in the refrigerator and will keep for several weeks.

EXTRA STRONG | STRONG | MEDIUM | MILD

KIMCHI AND PRAWN

FRIED RICE

ϱ ϱ ϱ ϱ

PREPARATION: 15 MINS / COOKING: APPROXIMATELY 20 MINS

SERVES 4

▪ 16 raw unpeeled prawns ▪ 2 carrots ▪ 80g (2¾oz) Kimchi (see page 49) ▪ 4 tablespoons sesame oil ▪ 300g (10½oz) cooked white rice ▪ 4 tablespoons soy sauce ▪ 1 spring onion ▪ 1 tablespoon sesame seeds ▪ Salt and freshly ground black pepper

---

1/ Remove the heads and shells of the prawns, taking care to keep the tails, and devein (remove the small black thread) using a sharp knife. Peel and finely dice the carrots. Roughly chop the kimchi.

2/ Heat 2 tablespoons sesame oil in a frying pan. Add the carrots and brown them for 5 minutes, stirring regularly. Add the prawns and let them brown for another 4 minutes, then remove them from the pan.

3/ In the same frying pan, heat 2 more tablespoons sesame oil. Add the rice and soy sauce. Stir-fry the rice over high heat for 3 or 4 minutes. Add the roughly chopped kimchi, prawns and carrots. Continue cooking for another 2 or 3 minutes.

4/ Chop the spring onion. Transfer the rice and prawns to a serving dish. Sprinkle with a little spring onion and sesame seeds. Adjust the seasoning and serve immediately.

EXTRA STRONG

STRONG

MEDIUM

◀

MILD

TIP
Be careful with the salt: kimchi and soy sauce are already salty.

KIMCHI JEON

(KIMCHI PANCAKE)

PREPARATION: 15 MINS / COOKING: 6 MINS

MAKES ABOUT 6 PANCAKES

- 200g (7oz) Kimchi (see page 49) • 2 spring onions with green stems • 1 egg
- 100g (3½oz) plain flour • 150ml (¼ pint) water • 2 tablespoons sunflower oil • Salt

---

1/ Roughly chop the kimchi without draining it. Finely chop the white bulb of the spring onions and some of the green stem.

2/ In a bowl, beat the egg with the flour. Pour in the measured water gradually. Add the kimchi, onions and 1 tablespoon oil. Season and mix well.

3/ Heat 1 tablespoon oil in a frying pan. Pour in a small ladleful of the mixture and cook over medium heat for about 3 minutes on each side, until the pancake is golden brown. Repeat with the rest of the mixture.

4/ Serve the pancakes warm or hot.

EXTRA STRONG | STRONG | MEDIUM | MILD

TIP
Be careful with the salt: kimchi is already salty.

GOCHUJANG

CHICKEN WINGS

ℓℓℓℓ

MARINATING: 2 HOURS / PREPARATION: 15 MINS / COOKING: 8 MINS

SERVES 4

- 8 chicken wings - 500ml (18fl oz) buttermilk - 50g (1¾oz) clear honey
- 50g (1¾oz) gochujang (Korean chilli paste) - 25ml (1fl oz) rice vinegar - 50g (1¾oz) ketchup - 1 teaspoon sesame oil - 50g (1¾oz) potato starch - 10g (¼oz) fast-action dried yeast - Frying oil - 3 fresh coriander sprigs, chopped - 1 tablespoon black and golden sesame seeds - Salt and freshly ground black pepper

---

1/ Cut the wings in half at the joint, then marinate them for 2 hours in the buttermilk.

2/ Meanwhile, prepare the sauce by mixing the honey, gochujang, rice vinegar, ketchup and sesame oil.

3/ Drain the wings and roughly dry them with kitchen paper. Place the potato starch and yeast in a shallow dish, mix well and coat the wings in the mixture.

4/ In a deep frying pan, heat enough frying oil to cover the wings to 180ºC (350ºF), or until a small piece of bread thrown into the oil browns in 30–40 seconds. Fry the wings for 7–8 minutes depending on their size.

5/ Drain the chicken wings on kitchen paper and coat them with the prepared sauce.

6/ Before serving, adjust the seasoning and sprinkle with chopped coriander and sesame seeds. Serve immediately.

EXTRA STRONG | STRONG | MEDIUM | MILD

PADRÓN PEPPER

10
—
9
—
8
—
7
—
6
—
5
—
▶ 4
—
3
—
2
—
1
—
0
—

SIZE
5cm (2 inches)

ORIGIN
This chilli pepper is said to have originated in Chile and was imported to Galicia, in Spain, in the 16th century by missionaries from the Franciscan monastery of Herbón, located in the village of Padrón.

WHERE IS IT EATEN?
It is found mainly in Spain.

EATING
It is eaten fried, sprinkled with sea salt flakes. The stalk is not removed for cooking but is not eaten.

PLANT
The green Padrón chilli pepper belongs to the nightshade family, specifically to the species *Capsicum annuum*.

The Padrón pepper takes its name from the village where the monastery is located; Padrón is in Galicia, in the province of A Coruña.

This pepper has PDO (protected designation of origin) status. It ranges in colour from bright green to yellowish green. It is elongated and conical in shape, with furrows.

Only 10 per cent of Padrón peppers are considered hot. Hence the saying, '*os pementos de Padrón, uns pican e outros non*' or 'Peppers from Padrón: some are hot, and some are not.'

Whether or not it is spicy depends on the climatic conditions in which it is cultivated. It is said that if the plant is watered from the ground, it will be a sweet pepper, and if its stem and leaves are watered, it will become hot.

If the pepper's shape is irregular, its skin is matte and it squeaks when you poke it with a finger, it is likely to be spicy.

The peppers are harvested between May and the end of summer. Saint Martin's Day, on 11 November, is the last date for it to appear at farmers' markets. However, greenhouse cultivation now allows the peppers to be sold year-round in supermarkets.

TIP
Be careful of splashing oil when cooking the chillies.

FRIED PADRÓN PEPPERS

WITH SEA SALT FLAKES

ϵϵϵϵ

PREPARATION: 2 MINS / COOKING: 4 MINS

SERVES 4

- 280g (10oz) Padrón chilli peppers
- 200ml (⅓ pint) olive oil • Sea salt flakes

1/ Wash and dry the chilli peppers well.

2/ Heat the olive oil in a deep frying pan, add the peppers and brown them for 3 or 4 minutes over high heat.

3/ Drain the peppers on kitchen paper and sprinkle generously with sea salt flakes.

4/ Serve immediately.

| EXTRA STRONG |

| STRONG |

| MEDIUM |

▶ | MILD |

ESPELETTE PEPPER

SIZE
7–14cm (2¾–5½ inches)

ORIGIN
This chilli pepper is originally from Mexico but it was recorded as early as 1650 in the Labourd region (former name of the Pyrénées-Atlantiques department) in France.

WHERE IS IT EATEN?
It is found in the Basque Country in Spain and throughout France.

EATING
Espelette pepper is found in many Basque culinary specialties such as axoa, piperade and Basque chicken. It also pairs very well with sweet flavours such as cocoa or tropical fruits.

PLANT
Espelette pepper belongs to the nightshade family and specifically to the species *Capsicum annuum*, the gorria variety.

It was initially cultivated because it was a good replacement for black pepper, which was very expensive at the time. It was therefore used for seasoning but it was also a means of preservation.

The Espelette pepper is rated 4 on the simplified Scoville scale.

It is conical in shape and is harvested by hand when it is red. Harvest begins in August and ends with the first frosts.

This is the only French spice that has both an AOC (*appellation d'origine contrôlée*) and a PDO (protected designation of origin) status.

Its transformation into powder requires several steps. Once picked, the pepper is strung on ropes to mature for 15 days. It is then gently dehydrated and the stalk is removed by hand. It is then dried again before being ground into a powder that can vary in fineness.

Espelette pepper is sold in three forms: fresh on strings, dried on strings or in powder form. Fresh chilli peppers in bulk are only sold for commercial processing.

TIP
You can add a veal bone to thicken the sauce.

VEAL STEW

ϲϲϲϲ

PREPARATION: 30 MINS / COOKING: 1 HOUR 40 MINS

SERVES 6

▪ 1 green sweet pepper ▪ 2 red sweet peppers ▪ 4 green chilli peppers ▪ 800g (1lb 12oz) small potatoes ▪ 5 spring onions with green stems ▪ 4 garlic cloves ▪ 5 ripe tomatoes or 227g (8oz) can of chopped tomatoes with juice ▪ 800g (1lb 12oz) veal shoulder ▪ 4 thyme sprigs (plus extra to garnish) ▪ 4 tablespoons extra virgin olive oil ▪ 2 bay leaves ▪ ½ teaspoon Espelette pepper ▪ 100ml (3½fl oz) sweet white wine ▪ 300ml (½ pint) veal stock ▪ Salt and freshly ground black pepper

---

Ovenproof casserole pot

1/ Wash and dry the sweet peppers and sweet green chilli peppers. Remove the stems, membranes and seeds. Finely dice the flesh.

2/ Peel the potatoes. Peel the garlic cloves. Finely chop the garlic and spring onions. Keep some of the green stem of the spring onions to garnish the final dish.

3/ Preheat the oven to 180°C fan (400°F), Gas Mark 6. Place the tomatoes in a bowl and pour over boiling water to cover. Leave for 1–2 minutes, then drain, cut a cross at the stem end of each tomato and peel off the skins. Remove the seeds and cut them into quarters.

4/ Dice the veal shoulder with a sharp knife. Strip the leaves from the thyme sprigs.

5/ In a large, deep frying pan, heat 2 tablespoons of extra virgin olive oil. Add the spring onions and garlic, sweet peppers, thyme and bay leaves. Brown for 5 minutes.

6/ At the same time, heat the remaining 2 tablespoons extra virgin olive oil in an ovenproof casserole pot and brown the veal over high heat for 5–6 minutes.

7/ Add the onions, garlic and sweet peppers to the casserole pot, then the potatoes (cut into pieces if they are large) and the tomatoes. Add salt and pepper, the Espelette pepper, white wine and veal stock.

8/ Cover and bake for 1½ hours.

9/ Just before serving, adjust the seasoning, scatter over a few of the chopped green spring onion stems and a few thyme sprigs and serve immediately.

EXTRA STRONG | STRONG | MEDIUM ▶ | MILD

CURED DUCK BREAST

WITH ESPELETTE PEPPER

🌶🌶🌶🌶

PREPARATION: 10 MINS / DEHYDRATION: 3 DAYS / MATURATION: 3-4 WEEKS

SERVES 4-6

▪ 1 duck breast ▪ 350g (12oz) coarse salt ▪ 1 tablespoon Espelette pepper
▪ 1 tablespoon thyme leaves

Large airtight container

1/ Dry the duck breast well using kitchen paper. Place half of the salt in an airtight container. Add the duck breast and cover it with the remaining salt. Seal tightly and refrigerate for 3 days.

2/ Remove most of the salt. Rinse the duck breast under cold running water to completely desalinate it. Dry it well.

3/ Mix the Espelette pepper and the thyme leaves, then spread them over the duck breast, skin side and flesh side.

4/ Wrap the duck breast in a clean cloth and store in the bottom of the refrigerator for at least 3 weeks.

5/ Cut the duck breast into thin slices and enjoy as an appetizer or in salads.

EXTRA STRONG | STRONG | MEDIUM | MILD

BASQUE
CHICKEN

PREPARATION: 20 MINS / COOKING: 45 MINS

SERVES 4

▪ 1 small chicken, about 1kg (2lb 4oz) ▪ 2 garlic cloves ▪ 2 onions ▪ 6 tomatoes or 400g (14oz) can of plum tomatoes ▪ 1 red sweet pepper ▪ 1 green sweet pepper ▪ 100ml (3½fl oz) white wine ▪ 1 tablespoon Espelette pepper ▪ 25g (1oz) butter ▪ 150ml (¼ pint) passata ▪ Salt

---

Heavy-based casserole pot

1/ Cut the chicken into 8 pieces. Peel the garlic cloves. Finely chop the garlic and onions.

2/ Wash and dry the tomatoes and sweet peppers and remove their stems. Remove the seeds and membranes from the sweet peppers. Cut the tomatoes into quarters and the sweet peppers into strips.

3/ In a heavy-based casserole pot, melt the butter. Add the chicken pieces and brown them on all sides for 5 minutes. Deglaze (use a liquid to loosen any pieces of food stuck to the bottom of a pan) with the white wine and continue cooking for another 2 or 3 minutes.

4/ Remove the chicken pieces and set them aside. Add the chopped onions and garlic, and the passata and cook for 3 or 4 minutes. Add the sweet peppers, tomatoes, Espelette pepper and chicken pieces, and season with salt. Cover and cook over a low heat for 35 minutes.

5/ Adjust the seasoning and serve immediately.

EXTRA STRONG | STRONG | MEDIUM | MILD

SERVING SUGGESTION
Serve with basmati rice.

TRUFFLES

WITH ESPELETTE PEPPER

ℓℓℓℓ

PREPARATION: 25 MINS / REFRIGERATION: 1 HOUR

MAKES ABOUT 35 TRUFFLES

▪ 150g (5½oz) milk couverture chocolate or cooking chocolate ▪ 150g (5½oz) dark couverture chocolate or cooking chocolate ▪ 150ml (¼ pint) double cream ▪ 50g (1¾oz) clear honey ▪ 1 teaspoon Espelette pepper ▪ 70g (2½oz) unsweetened cocoa powder

Smooth piping bag and plain nozzle ▪ Baking tray ▪ Nonstick baking paper

1/ Chop the milk and dark chocolate and place in a heatproof bowl.

2/ Pour the cream and honey into a saucepan and bring the mixture to the boil. Pour the cream mixture over the chocolate. Wait a few minutes and then stir gently to obtain a smooth ganache (silky mixture). Add the Espelette pepper and mix well. Place the ganache in the refrigerator for 30 minutes.

3/ Pour the ganache into a smooth piping bag. Line a baking tray with nonstick baking paper and then pipe small balls of ganache onto the paper. Chill in the refrigerator for 30 minutes.

4/ Roll the truffles quickly in your hands to smooth them off, then roll them in the unsweetened cocoa powder.

5/ Store the truffles in an airtight container in a cool place and consume within 5 days.

| EXTRA STRONG | · STRONG | MEDIUM | MILD |

SUBSTITUTIONS

You can replace homemade fish stock with commercial fish stock. In peak season, you can swap canned tomatoes for fresh tomatoes.

TUNA STEW

ϾϾϾϾ

PREPARATION: 15 MINS / COOKING: 55 MINS

SERVES 4

• 4 baby carrots • 1 garlic clove • 1 onion • 2 sweet green peppers • 280g (10oz) waxy potatoes (such as Charlotte) • 5 tablespoons olive oil • 100ml (3½fl oz) white cooking wine • 227g (8oz) can of chopped tomatoes • 1 teaspoon Espelette pepper • 300g (10½oz) tuna • 4 flat leaf parsley sprigs • Salt and freshly ground black pepper **FOR 500ML (18FL OZ) OF TUNA STOCK** • 3 tablespoons olive oil • 1 tuna head • 1 tuna bone • 1 bouquet garni (a bundle of herbs tied with string or in a small muslin bag) • 1 tablespoon coarse salt

Fine mesh sieve • Garlic press

1/ **PREPARE THE STOCK.** In a heavy-based saucepan, heat the olive oil. Add the tuna head and bone, the bouquet garni and the coarse salt. Cover with water, bring to the boil, cover and simmer for 30 minutes. Pass through a fine mesh sieve and set aside in a container.

2/ Peel the carrots. Peel the garlic clove and crush it. Finely chop the onion.

3/ Wash and dry the sweet peppers and potatoes. Cut the sweet peppers into 1cm (½ inch) pieces. Cut any larger potatoes in half.

4/ In a saucepan, heat 3 tablespoons olive oil and add the onion and garlic. Brown for a few minutes. Deglaze with the white wine to loosen any pieces of food stuck to the bottom of the pan. Add the chopped tomatoes, green sweet peppers, Espelette pepper, carrots, potatoes and the reserved fish stock. Adjust the seasoning. Cover and cook for 25 minutes, then remove from the heat.

5/ Cut the tuna into large cubes. Brown them for 2 minutes in a frying pan with the remaining 2 tablespoons oil.

6/ Add the browned tuna to the saucepan with the sauce, cover and let stand for 5 minutes: the tuna will finish cooking from the residual heat.

7/ Chop the parsley and sprinkle over the dish before serving piping hot.

EXTRA STRONG | STRONG | MEDIUM | MILD

PINEAPPLE CARPACCIO

WITH ESPELETTE PEPPER

PREPARATION: 10 MINS

SERVES 4

• 1 very cold Victoria pineapple or another pineapple with an edible core
• ½ teaspoon Espelette pepper

1/ Peel the pineapple and cut it into thin slices using a sharp knife.

2/ Divide the slices among 4 serving plates.

3/ Sprinkle with Espelette pepper.

4/ Serve immediately.

| EXTRA STRONG

| STRONG

| MEDIUM ▶

| MILD

ALEPPO CHILLI PEPPER

10

ORIGIN
This pepper is from the Aleppo region, in Syria.

9

WHERE IS IT EATEN?
It is a chilli pepper that is very prevalent in the Middle East and throughout the wider region from Turkey to Syria via Lebanon.

8

7

EATING
It is found in fattoush salad, menemen (vegetable and egg stew), labneh, tabbouleh, hummus, maklouba and kefta. Aleppo chilli pepper goes very well with sumac.

6

5

▶ **4**

PLANT
Aleppo chilli pepper belongs to the nightshade family, specifically to the species *Capsicum annuum*.

3

2

1

0

The Aleppo chilli pepper is also called Halaby pepper or Turkish pepper.

It is rated 4 on the simplified Scoville scale.

As it originates from the Aleppo region, on the Silk Road, it was very widely distributed across the region. Today, for geopolitical reasons, Aleppo chilli pepper is mainly grown in Turkey (in the province of Gaziantep).

Thanks to the soil and semi-arid climate of the Syrian plateau, the Aleppo chilli pepper has developed a dark red flesh. It is very fruity and almost sweet.

It is dried in the sun, crushed and then mixed with oil and salt. It is traditionally used in the form of flakes or slivers. It is rarely ground because this would spoil its flavours. Aleppo chilli pepper is used more as a spice or condiment than as a vegetable.

FATTOUSH SALAD

ϲϲϲϲ

PREPARATION: 15 MINS / COOKING: A FEW MINUTES

SERVES 4

• 2 Lebanese flatbreads • 4 tomatoes • 1 cucumber • 1 red onion • 4 Little Gem lettuces
• 1 unwaxed lemon • 8 tablespoons olive oil • 8 Kalamata olives, pitted • 1 teaspoon Aleppo
chilli flakes • Salt and freshly ground black pepper

Grater

1/ Brown the Lebanese flatbreads in a hot frying pan until they become crispy. Set aside.

2/ Wash the tomatoes and cucumber. Remove the stems from the tomatoes, cut them
into quarters and remove the seeds. Cut the cucumber in half lengthways and remove
the seeds. Finely dice the tomatoes and cucumber. Cut the onion into small pieces.
Separate the leaves of the Little Gem lettuces, rinse and dry them.

3/ Wash the lemon, zest it with the grater and then squeeze it. Mix the juice with the
olive oil, salt and black pepper.

4/ Mix all the salad ingredients, drizzle with lemon vinaigrette and sprinkle with the
Aleppo chilli pepper. Serve with the crunchy Lebanese bread cut into pieces.

| EXTRA STRONG |

| STRONG |

| MEDIUM |

| MILD

LEBANESE-STYLE TABBOULEH

ﻉﻉﻉﻉ

PREPARATION: 20 MINS / COOKING: 6 MINS

SERVES 4

- 80g (2¾oz) bulgur wheat ▪ 4 tomatoes ▪ ½ red sweet pepper ▪ ½ cucumber
- 1 large unwaxed lemon ▪ 4 spring onions ▪ 1 bunch of flat leaf parsley
- 1 bunch of mint ▪ 1 tablespoon Aleppo chilli pepper ▪ 6 tablespoons olive oil
- Salt and freshly ground black pepper

Grater

1/ Cook the bulgur wheat as indicated on the package and drain it.

2/ Wash the tomatoes, red sweet pepper, cucumber and lemon. Place the tomatoes in a bowl and pour over boiling water to cover. Leave for 1–2 minutes, then drain, cut a cross at the stem end of each tomato, and peel off the skins. Remove the seeds and crush them.

3/ Remove the stem, seeds and white membranes from the sweet pepper. Cut the flesh into small pieces. Remove the seeds from the cucumber and dice it finely. Zest the lemon with the grater and then squeeze it. Finely chop the onions. Wash, dry and strip the parsley and mint leaves, then chop them finely.

4/ Mix all the ingredients, adjust the seasoning and serve very cold.

EXTRA STRONG | STRONG | MEDIUM | MILD

SPICY LAMB MEATBALLS

ℓℓℓℓ

PREPARATION: 20 MINS / COOKING: 20–25 MINS

SERVES 4 (APPROXIMATELY 20 MEATBALLS)
▪ 2 garlic cloves ▪ 2 spring onions ▪ 4 mint sprigs ▪ 600g (1lb 5oz) minced lamb
▪ 1 teaspoon ground cumin ▪ 1 teaspoon curry powder ▪ ½ teaspoon Aleppo chilli pepper
▪ 2 tablespoons olive oil ▪ Salt

Garlic press ▪ Baking tray

1/ Preheat the oven to 180°C fan (400°F), Gas Mark 6. Peel the garlic cloves. Finely chop the spring onions and crush the garlic cloves using a garlic press. Wash, dry and strip the mint leaves. Chop them finely.

2/ Mix the meat, spring onions, garlic, mint, cumin, curry powder, Aleppo chilli pepper and olive oil. Add salt to taste.

3/ Moisten your hands and form the mixture into approximately 20 balls. Place them on the baking tray as you go.

4/ Bake for 20–25 minutes, turning the meatballs halfway through cooking.

EXTRA STRONG | STRONG | MEDIUM | MILD

JALAPEÑO

DRIED VERSION: CHIPOTLE

10 —

9 —

8 —

7 —

6 —

▶ 5 —

4 —

3 —

2 —

1 —

0 —

SIZE
5–9cm (2–3½ inches)

ORIGIN
The jalapeño gets its name from its place of origin, Xalapa, a city in the state of Veracruz located in eastern Mexico.

WHERE IS IT EATEN?
It is found mainly in Mexico and the USA but also in Asia in the form of sriracha sauce.

EATING
Jalapeño chilli peppers are eaten whole and grilled, stuffed with cheese in *huevos de armadillo*, or sliced on meat. Chipotle is used to infuse sauces or oils when used whole or to add spice to dishes when used in ground form. It also pairs very well with chocolate or eggs.

PLANT
The plant can grow up to 1 metre (3ft) and each plant yields about 30 peppers. The jalapeño pepper belongs to the nightshade family, specifically to the species *Capsicum annuum*.

It is rated 4–5 on the simplified Scoville scale.

The jalapeño pepper has a fruity and spicy taste. As it matures, the colour changes from green to red. The riper it is, the spicier it is.

The name chipotle derives from the process whereby the pepper is dried and then smoked using pecan wood, a method that dates back to the time of the Aztecs.

The chipotle chilli pepper (*chi* means 'chilli pepper' and *poctli* means 'smoked') has a strong, smoky flavour, quite sweet with notes of nuts, chocolate and hazelnuts. It is one of the most frequently used peppers in Mexico and the most used in the United States.

It is found in different forms: ground, as a sauce and whole in cans.

SRIRACHA-GLAZED SALMON

ʕ ʕ ʕ ʕ

PREPARATION: 15 MINS / MARINATING: 2 HOURS / COOKING: 20–25 MINS

SERVES 4

• 4 fairly thick salmon fillets, about 800g (1lb 12oz) • 1 small bunch of thyme
FOR THE MARINADE • 4 tablespoons sriracha sauce (see page 193) • 3 tablespoons clear
honey • 3 tablespoons soy sauce • 3 tablespoons olive oil • Freshly ground black pepper

Baking tray • Nonstick baking paper

1/ **PREPARE THE MARINADE.** In a shallow dish, combine the sriracha sauce, honey, soy
sauce and olive oil. Season with black pepper.

2/ Rinse the salmon fillets under cold water and dry them with kitchen paper. Remove
the skin from the salmon and cut the fish into large cubes. Add it to the marinade and
coat well. Cover and refrigerate for at least 2 hours. Strip the leaves from the thyme.

3/ Preheat the oven to 180°C fan (400°F), Gas Mark 6. Place the salmon pieces on a
baking tray lined with baking paper, taking care that they do not touch each other.
Bake for 20–25 minutes depending on the size of the cubes, pouring over a little
marinade halfway through cooking.

4/ Serve hot with fresh thyme leaves sprinkled over.

EXTRA STRONG

STRONG

MEDIUM ▶

MILD

HUEVOS RANCHEROS

ℰℰℰℰ

PREPARATION: 20 MINS / COOKING: 20 MINS

SERVES 4

- 4 tomatoes - 1 garlic clove - 2 red jalapeño chilli peppers - 1 onion
- 5 tablespoons olive oil - 4 eggs - 4 corn or wheat tortillas - 1 spring onion - Salt

Blender

1/ Using a sharp knife, make a cross on the tomatoes opposite the stem. Peel the garlic clove. Bring a large saucepan of salted water to the boil. Add the tomatoes, garlic clove and the 2 chilli peppers and boil for 10 minutes.

2/ Meanwhile, finely chop the onion. Heat 3 tablespoons of olive oil in a pan, add the onion and brown over low heat for 10 minutes.

3/ Drain the tomatoes, chilli peppers and garlic. Remove the stems from the chilli peppers and tomatoes. Place the tomatoes in a bowl and pour over boiling water to cover. Leave for 1–2 minutes, then drain, cut a cross at the stem end of each tomato, and peel off the skins. Remove the seeds. Cut the chilli peppers in half and remove the membranes and seeds. Using a small blender, very finely chop the tomatoes, garlic and chilli peppers.

4/ Add the blended chilli paste to the pan with the onion. Season and simmer for 10 minutes over low heat.

5/ Meanwhile, fry 4 eggs in the remaining olive oil. Heat the tortillas in a dry frying pan.

6/ Place a tortilla on each serving plate. Top each one with an egg and spread the sauce all around.

7/ Wash, dry and chop the spring onion, sprinkle over the dish and serve immediately.

EXTRA STRONG

STRONG

MEDIUM ▶

MILD

TIP
It is quite difficult to find fresh tomatillos, but you can easily find them canned in South American grocery shops or online.

ENCHILADA

AND SALSA VERDE

ᥫᥫᥫᥫ

PREPARATION: 20 MINS / COOKING: 50 MINS

SERVES 4

- 3 chicken breasts - 1 bouquet garni (a bundle of herbs tied with string
or in a small muslin bag) - 12 small corn tortillas
FOR THE SALSA VERDE - 2 garlic cloves - 1 onion - 2 green jalapeño chilli peppers
- 500g (1lb 2oz) fresh or canned tomatillos - ½ bunch of fresh coriander - Salt
FOR THE BECHAMEL - 20g (¾oz) butter - 20g (¾oz) flour - 300ml (½ pint) milk
- 40g (1½oz) grated mozzarella-type cheese
FOR THE GRATIN - 40g (1½oz) grated mozzarella-type cheese

Blender

1/ Poach the chicken breasts for 30 minutes in a large saucepan of water with the bouquet garni.

2/ **MEANWHILE, PREPARE THE SALSA VERDE.** Peel the garlic cloves. Cut the onion into quarters. Remove the stems, seeds and membranes from the chilli peppers. Bring a large saucepan of water to the boil and add the tomatillos, chilli peppers, onion and garlic cloves. Simmer for 15 minutes. Drain, add the coriander and blend, then adjust the seasoning.

3/ Drain the chicken breasts. Let them cool and shred them.

4/ **MAKE THE BECHAMEL.** Melt the butter in a small saucepan then remove from the heat and add the flour in one go. Return to the heat, stirring with a wooden spoon, and cook for a few minutes. Pour in the milk and whisk continuously until the béchamel thickens slightly. Stir in the cheese and set aside.

5/ Preheat the oven to 180°C fan (400°F), Gas Mark 6. Dip each tortilla in the salsa verde and drain. Scatter a little chicken across the tortillas and roll them up. Place them in a baking dish as you go. Cover with the remaining salsa verde and then with béchamel. Sprinkle with grated cheese and bake for 20 minutes until well browned.

EXTRA STRONG | STRONG | MEDIUM | MILD

CHIPOTLE
SCRAMBLED EGG BOATS

ℓℓℓℓ

PREPARATION: 5 MINS / RESTING: 1 HOUR / COOKING: APPROXIMATELY 6–8 MINS

SERVES 4

- 1 chipotle chilli pepper - 4 eggs - 2 tablespoons double cream - 1 Little Gem lettuce
- 2 pinches of chipotle pepper powder - 2 fresh coriander sprigs - Salt

---

1/ Remove the stalk, seeds and membranes from the chipotle chilli pepper. Cut the flesh into strips.

2/ Beat the eggs in a bowl. Add the cream, chilli strips and salt, to taste. Mix well and let it infuse in a cool place for 1 hour.

3/ Meanwhile, separate the leaves of the Little Gem lettuce, rinse well and dry them. Chop the coriander.

4/ Remove the chilli strips from the creamy egg mixture. Scramble the eggs in a bain-marie, stirring constantly. (Heat a small saucepan of water. Place the bowl with the egg mixture over the pan so that the bottom of the bowl does not touch the water.)

5/ Divide the scrambled eggs among the lettuce leaves, sprinkle with the chilli powder and top with chopped coriander.

6/ Serve immediately.

EXTRA STRONG

STRONG

MEDIUM ▶

MILD

PAPRIKA

10	

SIZE
4–5cm (1½–2 inches)

ORIGIN
This pepper is from Central and South America.

WHERE IS IT EATEN?
It is found mainly in Hungary but it is consumed all over Europe and particularly in Spain in its smoked version.

EATING
This pepper should not be over-roasted, otherwise it will become bitter.

Sweet paprika is Hungary's star spice and is found in the national dish, goulash. Smoked paprika is popular in Spain and can be found, among other things, in the recipe for Octopus Galician style (see page 89).

PLANT
Paprika belongs to the nightshade family, specifically to the species *Capsicum annuum*.

Paprika is rated 0–5 on the Scoville scale.

You may see references to sweet paprika or hot paprika. They can also be distinguished by referring to Hungarian paprika, a pepper which is sweet because it is made only from the dried and crushed fruit, or royal paprika, a hot paprika made by crushing the fruit, the grains and the stems.

Paprika was introduced to Europe during the Spanish colonization of South America. It enjoyed such popularity in Spain that it was nicknamed 'Spanish pepper'.

There is also a smoky and spicy version of paprika better known as *pimentón de la Vera*. This smoked chilli pepper has PDO (protected designation of origin) status and is grown exclusively in the Cáceres region of Spain. It is dried then smoked with holm oak wood before being ground on a stone mill.

GOULASH

ℓℓℓℓ

PREPARATION: 30 MINS / COOKING: 2 HOURS 10 MINS

SERVES 4-6

▪ 1 garlic clove ▪ 2 large onions ▪ 4 firm-fleshed type potatoes (such as Charlotte) ▪ 2 carrots ▪ 1 red sweet pepper ▪ 227g (8oz) can of plum tomatoes ▪ 600g (1lb 5oz) stewing beef (chuck type) ▪ 2 tablespoons olive oil ▪ 15g (½oz) butter ▪ 2 teaspoons sweet paprika ▪ ½ teaspoon ground cumin ▪ 70g (2½oz) tomato purée ▪ 200ml (⅓ pint) red table wine ▪ 1.2 litres (2 pints) beef stock ▪ 3 or 4 chervil sprigs

Heavy-based casserole pot

1/ Peel the garlic clove. Finely chop the garlic and onions. Peel the potatoes and carrots, then cut the potatoes into cubes and the carrots into slices.

2/ Rinse the sweet pepper under cold water, dry it and cut it into thin strips, removing the membranes and seeds. Deseed the tomatoes and cut them into quarters. Cut the meat into approximately 2cm (¾ inch) cubes.

3/ In a heavy-based casserole pot, heat the oil and butter. Add the meat and let it brown over high heat for 5 minutes, stirring from time to time. Remove it from the casserole pot. Add the chopped garlic and onion to the casserole pot along with the paprika and ground cumin. Brown for 3 or 4 minutes, then put the meat back in the casserole pot along with the carrots and sweet pepper, tomato purée, tomatoes, wine and beef stock. Simmer for 2 hours. Add the potatoes 30 minutes before the end of cooking.

4/ Wash and chop the chervil. Adjust the seasoning and sprinkle the goulash with chervil.

| EXTRA STRONG |

| STRONG |

| MEDIUM |

| MILD |

◀

SUBSTITUTION
If you like spicy food, you can substitute 1 teaspoon of the sweet paprika with 1 teaspoon of hot paprika.

OCTOPUS

GALICIAN STYLE

ℓℓℓℓ

PREPARATION: 20 MINS / COOKING: 45 MINS

SERVES 4

- 1 defrosted octopus (see Tip, below), about 1kg (2lb 4oz) - 4 potatoes
- 6 tablespoons olive oil - 1 teaspoon hot or smoked paprika - Sea salt flakes

---

1/ Remove the head of the octopus by cutting at the point where it meets the tentacles. Remove the small hard beak. Clean the tentacles well with a small brush to remove any impurities in the suckers.

2/ Bring a large saucepan of unsalted water to the boil and immerse the octopus in the water for 5 seconds and then remove it. Repeat the process 3 times, waiting 10 seconds between each dunking. After the third time, put the octopus back in the water and cook for 25 minutes. Turn off the heat and leave the octopus in the water for another 20 minutes.

3/ Meanwhile, cook the potatoes for 25 minutes in a large saucepan of salted boiling water. Drain, peel and then cut them into slices 1cm (½ inch) thick.

4/ Cut the octopus tentacles into sections ½cm (¼ inch) thick. Cut the rest of the octopus into small pieces.

5/ Place the potato slices on a plate (traditionally a wooden plate) and place the octopus pieces on top. Drizzle with olive oil and sprinkle with paprika and coarse salt flakes.

6/ Serve immediately.

| EXTRA STRONG |

| STRONG |

▶ | MEDIUM |

| MILD |

TIP
It is important that the octopus has been frozen so that it does not go rubbery.

ROASTED CAULIFLOWER CASSEROLE

WITH PAPRIKA

ϲϲϲϲ

PREPARATION: 15 MINS / COOKING: 1½ HOURS

SERVES 4–6

▪ 1 unwaxed lemon ▪ 3 garlic cloves ▪ 6 tablespoons olive oil ▪ 1 tablespoon smoked paprika ▪ 1 teaspoon ground coriander ▪ 1 cauliflower, about 800g (1lb 12oz) ▪ 4 thyme sprigs ▪ 1 red onion ▪ 227g (8oz) can of chopped tomatoes ▪ 200ml (⅓ pint) vegetable stock ▪ Salt and freshly ground black pepper

---

Grater ▪ Garlic press or pestle and mortar ▪ Ovenproof casserole pot

---

1/ Wash the lemon, zest it with the grater and then squeeze it. Peel the garlic cloves and crush them using a garlic press or pestle and mortar. Mix the crushed garlic, 4 tablespoons olive oil, smoked paprika, coriander and lemon zest until you have a smooth paste. Season with salt and pepper.

2/ Preheat the oven to 200°C fan (425°F), Gas Mark 7. Wash and dry the cauliflower and remove the leaves, then trim the base if necessary so that it is stable in the casserole pot. Coat the cauliflower with the spice paste (you can use disposable gloves).

3/ Strip the leaves from the thyme sprigs. Finely chop the onion. Mix it with the chopped tomatoes, thyme leaves, vegetable stock and remaining 2 tablespoons olive oil. Season with salt and black pepper.

4/ Pour this mixture into the ovenproof casserole pot. Place the cauliflower in the centre. Cover and bake for 1½ hours.

5/ Just before serving, sprinkle the cauliflower with lemon juice and serve immediately.

EXTRA STRONG | STRONG | MEDIUM | MILD

JAMBALAYA

WITH PRAWNS AND SMOKED SAUSAGE

ϲϲϲϲ

PREPARATION: 15 MINS / COOKING: 35–40 MINS

SERVES 4

▪ 1 garlic clove ▪ 1 onion ▪ 2 small carrots ▪ 1 sweet green pepper ▪ 2 smoked pork sausages
▪ 12 large unpeeled raw prawns ▪ 4 thyme sprigs ▪ 3 tablespoons olive oil ▪ 1 teaspoon
Cajun seasoning ▪ 1½ teaspoons smoked paprika ▪ 227g (8oz) can of chopped tomatoes
▪ 1 litre (1¾ pints) chicken stock ▪ 2 tablespoons tomato purée ▪ 150g (5½oz) long grain
basmati rice ▪ Salt and freshly ground black pepper

1/ Peel the garlic clove. Finely chop the garlic and onion.

2/ Peel the carrots and cut them into 1cm (½ inch) slices. Wash and dry the sweet
green pepper and cut it into ½cm (¼ inch) pieces.

3/ Cut the sausages into slices 1cm (½ inch) thick. Peel the prawns, taking care to
keep the tail, and devein (remove the small black thread) using a sharp knife.

4/ Strip the leaves from the thyme sprigs. In a large, deep frying pan, heat the olive
oil. Add the onion and garlic, brown for 3 minutes then add the pieces of sausage.
Continue cooking for another 5 minutes. Add the carrots, sweet green pepper, thyme,
Cajun seasoning and smoked paprika, chopped tomatoes, chicken stock, tomato
purée and rice.

5/ Mix well and cook over low heat for 25 minutes, add the prawns and continue
cooking for another 5 minutes. The rice should be tender.

6/ Serve hot.

EXTRA STRONG | STRONG | MEDIUM | MILD

TIP
The cod will release a lot of water and decrease in volume, so do not make the pieces too small.

COD KEBABS

WITH CHERMOULA SAUCE

ℓ ℓ ℓ ℓ

PREPARATION: 20 MINS / MARINATING: 2 HOURS / COOKING: 20–25 MINS

SERVES 4 (8 KEBABS)
▪ 1 cod loin, about 1kg (2lb 4oz) ▪ 16 cherry tomatoes
FOR THE CHERMOULA SAUCE ▪ 20 fresh coriander sprigs ▪ 20 flat leaf parsley sprigs
▪ 3 garlic cloves ▪ 1 tablespoon ground cumin ▪ 1 tablespoon hot paprika ▪ 4 tablespoons
lemon juice ▪ 130ml (4½fl oz) olive oil ▪ Salt and freshly ground black pepper

---

Blender ▪ 8 wooden skewers, soaked in water ▪ Baking tray ▪ Nonstick baking paper

---

1/ **PREPARE THE CHERMOULA SAUCE.** Wash, dry and strip the coriander and parsley.
Peel the garlic cloves. Using a small blender, finely chop the herbs and garlic. Add
the cumin, paprika, lemon juice and olive oil. Season with salt and pepper. Blend well.

2/ Wash and dry the cod loin. Cut it into large cubes and place them in a deep dish.
Add the chermoula sauce and coat the fish pieces in it. Leave to marinate for at
least 2 hours.

3/ Preheat the oven to 200°C fan (425°F), Gas Mark 7. Pierce the pieces of fish onto the
wooden skewers, alternating with cherry tomatoes. Place the skewers on a baking
tray lined with nonstick baking paper. Bake for 20–25 minutes depending on the size
of the pieces.

4/ Serve hot or cold.

EXTRA STRONG | STRONG | MEDIUM | MILD

CALABRIAN CHILLI PEPPER

10

SIZE
2–6cm (¾–2½ inches)

9

ORIGIN
This chilli pepper is grown in
Calabria, in Italy, also known
8
as the 'land of red gold'.

WHERE IS IT EATEN?
7
It is found mainly in Italy but easily
sourced across Europe, in flake
form, in Italian grocery shops.

6

EATING
It can be used in pizza oil,
▶ 5
in soup or in sauce for pasta
all'arrabbiata.

4

PLANT
The plant grows up to 80cm
(32 inches). The Calabrian chilli
3
pepper belongs to the nightshade
family, specifically to the species
Capsicum annuum.

2

1

0

Calabrian chilli pepper is also called *diavoletti rossi*, *peperoncino* or *piparedduzzu* in the local Italian dialect.

It is rated 5 on the simplified Scoville scale.

The Calabrian chilli pepper turns from green to red when fully ripe, with deep fruity flavours.

It can be found whole (fresh or dried), in flakes or in powder form.

PASTA

ALL'ARRABBIATA

ₑₑₑₑ

PREPARATION: 5 MINS / COOKING: 15 MINS

SERVES 4

▪ 2 garlic cloves ▪ 8 flat leaf parsley sprigs ▪ 2 dried Calabrian chilli peppers
▪ 4 tablespoons olive oil ▪ 400g (14oz) can of chopped tomatoes
▪ 320g (11½oz) spaghetti ▪ Salt **TO SERVE** ▪ Grated Pecorino or Parmesan cheese

---

Garlic press

1/ Peel the garlic cloves and crush them using a garlic press. Wash, dry and strip the parsley leaves, then chop finely. Remove the stems and seeds from the chilli peppers and chop the flesh coarsely.

2/ In a deep frying pan, heat the olive oil, add the garlic and cook gently for 2 or 3 minutes. Add the tomatoes, chilli peppers and half of the parsley. Simmer over low heat for 15 minutes. Add a little water if the sauce becomes too thick.

3/ Meanwhile, bring a large saucepan of salted water to the boil and cook the pasta al dente (according to the instructions on the package). Drain the pasta, reserving 1 ladleful of the cooking water.

4/ Add the pasta to the frying pan, along with the cooking water and the remaining parsley. Adjust the seasoning and stir to combine.

5/ Serve with Parmesan or Pecorino to sprinkle over.

| EXTRA STRONG |

| STRONG ▶

| MEDIUM |

| MILD |

PASTA

WITH CALABRIAN CHILLI PEPPER

ɛɛɛɛ

PREPARATION: 10 MINS / COOKING: APPROXIMATELY 9 MINS

SERVES 4

• 320g (11½oz) pasta of your choice • 2 garlic cloves
• 2 or 3 Calabrian chilli peppers • 8 tablespoons good quality olive oil • Salt
TO SERVE • Grated Pecorino or Parmesan cheese

Garlic press

1/ Cook the pasta al dente (according to the instructions on the package).

2/ Peel the garlic cloves and crush them using a garlic press. Roughly crush the Calabrian chilli peppers.

3/ In a deep frying pan, heat the oil, add the garlic cloves and chillies and cook gently for 5 minutes over low heat.

4/ Drain the pasta, taking care to keep a little of the cooking water. Pour the pasta into the frying pan and add the cooking water. Add salt and mix well.

5/ Serve immediately with Pecorino or Parmesan to sprinkle over.

EXTRA STRONG | STRONG | MEDIUM | MILD

TIP
Be careful not to burn the garlic and chilli as this will make your sauce bitter.

CHILLI OIL

PREPARATION: 10 MINS / INFUSION: 12 HOURS

MAKES 1 × 500ML (18FL OZ) BOTTLE

• 500ml (18fl oz) olive oil • 15 Calabrian chilli peppers • 5 thyme sprigs • 1 bay leaf

---

Sterilized glass bottle

1/ Pour the oil into a saucepan, add the chillies, thyme and bay leaf then bring to a simmer. Remove from the heat and leave to cool.

2/ Cover and leave to infuse for 12 hours.

3/ Pour into a sterilized, airtight bottle.

4/ Store in a cool, dark place. This keeps for several weeks.

EXTRA STRONG

STRONG

MEDIUM

MILD

TIP
Choose a dark coloured glass olive oil bottle, if you can, to protect the oil from light. This will help the oil keep for longer.

TAKANOTSUME

10

9

8

7

▶ 6

5

4

3

2

1

0

SIZE
4–5cm (1½–2 inches)

ORIGIN
It is native to South and
Central America.

WHERE IS IT EATEN?
It is found mainly in Japan but
is also easily sourced in Asian
grocery shops.

EATING
It is used in pickle recipes and
in meat stews.

PLANT
This variety of chilli pepper
is a plant that measures
approximately 50cm (20 inches)
in height. It produces abundant
clusters of pointed fruits that
ripen from light green to red.

This chilli pepper is the hottest of all the
Japanese chilli peppers.

It is rated 5–6 on the simplified Scoville scale.

Christopher Columbus introduced the
takanotsume chilli pepper to Europe in the
15th century and it is believed to have arrived
in Japan around the 16th century.

This chilli pepper is also known as hawk claw
because of its shape.

When the chilli pepper is eaten in its dried
form, it is called *ichimi togarashi*; when mixed
with other spices, it is called *shichimi togarashi*,
and when mixed with yuzu peel, it is called
yuzu kosho.

SPICY CHICKEN

WITH SAKE AND PAK CHOI

ƐƐƐƐ

PREPARATION: 20 MINS / COOKING: 25 MINS

SERVES 4

• 4 chicken thighs • 2 tablespoons plain flour • 2 tablespoons sake • 2cm (¾ inch) piece of
fresh root ginger • 2 garlic cloves • 1 leek • 4 small pak choi • 1 takanotsume chilli pepper
• 1 tablespoon oyster sauce • 1 tablespoon soy sauce • 1 tablespoon gochujang
(Korean chilli paste) • 1 tablespoon caster sugar • 2 tablespoons sesame oil
• Salt and freshly ground black pepper

Garlic press • Grater

1/ Debone the chicken thighs and mix the meat with the flour, sake, salt and pepper.
Put aside in the refrigerator.

2/ Peel the ginger and garlic cloves. Crush the garlic cloves using a garlic press and
grate the ginger.

3/ Cut the leek (white part only) into slices of about 1cm (½ inch). Cut the pak choi into
quarters lengthways and clean them well under running water. Chop the takanotsume
chilli pepper and mix it with the oyster sauce, soy sauce, gochujang and sugar.

4/ In a pan, heat the sesame oil. Add the ginger, garlic and chicken and brown for
4 minutes, turning the chicken pieces regularly. Add the leek and let it brown
for another 5 minutes.

5/ Pour in the chilli sauce mixture, 100ml (3½fl oz) of water and the pieces of pak choi
and simmer, covered, for 15–20 minutes.

EXTRA STRONG

STRONG ▶

MEDIUM

MILD

AJÍ AMARILLO

10 —

9 —

8 —

7 —

▶ 6 —

5 —

4 —

3 —

2 —

1 —

0 —

SIZE
10–18cm (4–7 inches)

ORIGIN
It originates from the Andes, from the city of Cuzco in Peru.

WHERE IS IT EATEN?
Ají amarillo is found mainly in Latin America. It can be easily sourced in Europe in frozen form.

EATING
It can be used fresh or dried (the seeds are removed), chopped or ground, in soups, marinades and stir-fries. It is very versatile and goes with everything.

It is found in many Peruvian dishes including ceviches, tiraditos, causa and *ají de gallina*. It is also used to make a paste that is a component of the famous huancaïna sauce.

PLANT
The ají amarillo chilli pepper belongs to the nightshade family, specifically to the species *Capsicum baccatum*.

It is rated 5–6 on the simplified Scoville scale.

The ají amarillo chilli pepper is an ancient variety cultivated in the Andes for centuries, producing green fruits that turn orange when fully ripe.

It is fairly strong but very fruity. It has a distinctive orange colour.

It can be cooked fresh but also dried. It is advisable to use gloves when handling it.

In Peru, all chilli peppers are called *ají*.

TIPS
'Soda crackers' are typical Peruvian crackers. They are easily found in South American grocery shops or online. If you cannot find them, a salty cracker like Ritz will do just as well. To protect your hands, wear gloves when handling hot chilli peppers.

CASSAVA FRIES

AND HUANCAÏNA SAUCE

ʕ ʕ ʕ ʕ

PREPARATION: 15 MINS / COOKING: 25 MINS

SERVES 4

FOR THE CASSAVA FRIES ▪ 800g cassava root ▪ 1 litre (1¾ pints) frying oil
FOR THE HUANCAÏNA SAUCE ▪ 2½ ají amarillo chilli peppers ▪ ½ red onion
▪ 2 tablespoons sunflower oil ▪ 4 soda crackers (see Tip, page 108)
▪ 100ml (3½fl oz) milk ▪ 100g (3½oz) soft cream cheese ▪ Salt

---

Disposable gloves ▪ Blender

1/ MAKE THE HUANCAÏNA SAUCE. Wash and dry the ají amarillo chilli peppers. Remove the stalks. Remove the seeds, membranes and filaments, then cut the flesh into strips. Finely chop the onion.

2/ In a frying pan, heat the sunflower oil. Add the chilli peppers and onion. Cover and cook for 15 minutes over low heat. Stir regularly so that the mixture does not colour.

3/ Using a blender, mix the chilli and onion, crackers, milk and soft cheese. Adjust the seasoning. Pour the sauce into a bowl and let it cool.

4/ MEANWHILE, MAKE THE CASSAVA FRIES. Peel the cassava, remove its fibrous central part then cut it into pieces approximately 8cm (3¼ inch) long and 1cm (½ inch) wide. Cook for 5 minutes in salted boiling water. Drain and then dry the pieces well using kitchen paper.

5/ Heat the frying oil in a sauté pan or a deep frying pan to 180°C (350°F), or until a small piece of bread thrown into the oil browns in 30–40 seconds. Dip the cassava fries into the hot oil and let them brown for about 3 or 4 minutes.

6/ Drain the fries on kitchen paper, and serve them with the huancaïna sauce.

EXTRA STRONG | STRONG | MEDIUM | MILD

TIP
Panquita is a Peruvian spice preparation sold in sachets; it is a bit like chicken stock powder. You can easily find it in South American grocery shops or online. An alternative is ancho chilli pepper (see page 38).

HAKE SUDADO (STEW)

WITH AJÍ AMARILLO CHILLI PEPPER

ℓℓℓℓ

PREPARATION: 20 MINS / COOKING: 35 MINS

SERVES 4

▪ 2 ají amarillo chilli peppers ▪ 2 tomatoes ▪ 4 fresh coriander sprigs ▪ 1 garlic clove ▪ 1 onion ▪ 1 lime ▪ 2 tablespoons neutral oil ▪ 1 × 30g (1oz) sachet of panquita (see Tip, page 110) ▪ 1 teaspoon ground cumin ▪ ½ teaspoon salt ▪ ½ teaspoon freshly ground black pepper ▪ 4 hake steaks ▪ 200ml (⅓ pint) dry white wine ▪ 200ml (⅓ pint) fish stock ▪ 3 tablespoons amarillo chilli paste from a sachet

---

Disposable gloves ▪ Heavy-based casserole pot

1/ Wash and dry the ají amarillo chilli peppers, tomatoes and coriander. Remove the stems from the tomatoes and cut them into small pieces. Strip the coriander leaves and chop them finely. Peel the garlic clove. Finely chop the garlic and onion. Remove the stems from the ají amarillo chilli peppers, as well as the seeds and filaments. Cut the flesh into strips. Squeeze the lime.

2/ In a heavy-based casserole pot, heat the oil. Add the onion, garlic and chillies. Brown for 5 minutes. Add the panquita, cumin, salt, pepper, fish, white wine, tomatoes, fish stock, sliced ají amarillo chilli peppers and amarillo chilli paste. Cover and simmer for 30 minutes, adding a little more fish stock if the sauce dries out too quickly.

3/ Sprinkle with lime juice and coriander. Serve immediately.

EXTRA STRONG | STRONG | MEDIUM | MILD

TABASCO®

10	
—	**SIZE** 3–5cm (1¼–2 inches)
9	
—	**ORIGIN** It is originally from Mexico, from the state of Tabasco.
8	
—	
	WHERE IS IT EATEN? Tabasco® sauce can be found all over the world.
▶ 7	
—	
6	**EATING** Tabasco® is used in particular in chilli con carne, steak tartare,
—	
5	tacos and Bloody Mary cocktails.
—	
	PLANT The plant is a dense shrub that
4	can produce up to 200 fruits.
—	The Tabasco chilli pepper
3	belongs to the nightshade family, specifically to the
—	species *Capsicum frutescens*.
2	
—	
1	
—	
0	
—	

It is rated 7 on the simplified Scoville scale.

The Tabasco is a small conical chilli pepper.

It is used to prepare the famous Tabasco® hot sauce. Fun fact: the Tabasco® harvesters use a little red wooden stick. It is a visual benchmark for harvesting the chilli peppers. Only those that are the same colour as the stick are harvested. The chilli peppers are stored straight away in wooden barrels with salt and vinegar. They macerate for 3 years, then the liquid is filtered and bottled.

BLOODY MARY

COCKTAIL

ℓℓℓℓ

PREPARATION: 5 MINS

SERVES 4

▪ 300ml (½ pint) tomato juice ▪ 150ml (¼ pint) vodka ▪ 4 teaspoons lemon juice
▪ 1 tablespoon Tabasco® sauce ▪ 1 tablespoon Worcestershire sauce
▪ ½ teaspoon celery salt

Shaker ▪ 4 tumbler glasses or cocktail glasses ▪ 8-12 ice cubes

---

1/ Put all the ingredients in a shaker with the ice cubes.

2/ Shake well and serve immediately in glasses filled with ice cubes.

EXTRA STRONG

STRONG ◀

MEDIUM

MILD

TIP
Have the celery salt and Tabasco® available for your guests. They can add more depending
on their chilli tolerance.

BEEF TARTARE

WITH TABASCO®

ƐƐƐƐ

PREPARATION: 15 MINS

SERVES 4

- 480g (1lb 1oz) beef fillet • 1 large shallot • 2 tablespoons chopped flat leaf parsley
• 4 tablespoons mayonnaise • 4 tablespoons capers • 4 tablespoons Worcestershire sauce
• 1 tablespoon Tabasco® sauce • Salt and freshly ground black pepper

---

1/ Cut up the meat into small dice with a knife. Peel and slice the shallot.

2/ Mix all the ingredients together and adjust the seasoning to taste.

3/ Serve immediately or keep chilled until ready to serve.

| EXTRA STRONG

| STRONG

| MEDIUM

| MILD

SERVING SUGGESTION
Serve with sweet potato or potato fries.

TOMATO CARPACCIO

WITH TABASCO® VINAIGRETTE

ℓℓℓℓ

PREPARATION: 5 MINS

SERVES 4

- 8 multicoloured tomatoes - 4 teaspoons olive oil - 1 teaspoon clear honey
- 1 tablespoon Tabasco® sauce - 2 tablespoons lemon juice - 2 chervil sprigs

---

1/ Wash and dry the tomatoes. Using a very sharp knife, cut them into thin slices.

2/ Mix the olive oil, honey, Tabasco® and the lemon juice in a jug.

3/ Drizzle the dressing over the carpaccio, sprinkle with the chervil leaves and serve immediately.

EXTRA STRONG

STRONG

MEDIUM

MILD

CHI-CHIEN CHILLI PEPPER

10
—
9
—
8 ▶
—
7
—
6
—
5
—
4
—
3
—
2
—
1
—
0
—

SIZE
6–7cm (2½–2¾ inches)

ORIGIN
This chilli pepper is from China.

WHERE IS IT EATEN?
It is found mainly in China.

EATING
It is eaten fresh or dried. It is found, for example, in Sichuan mapo tofu or in roast pork with spices and pineapple.

PLANT
Its plant is compact and measures approximately 60cm (24 inches) high, with dark green foliage and stems. It is a Chinese variety with small red fruits growing in tight, upward-pointing clusters. This chilli pepper has a thin skin, making it easy to dry. It changes from green to red in about 80 days.

The chi-chien chilli pepper belongs to the nightshade family, specifically to the species *Capsicum annuum*. Chi-chien is a hot chilli pepper.

It is rated 8 on the simplified Scoville scale.

SERVING SUGGESTION
Serve with white rice.

CHINESE-STYLE PORK

ℓℓℓℓ

PREPARATION: 20 MINS / COOKING: 1½ HOURS

SERVES 4

- ½ pineapple - 1 chi-chien chilli pepper - 50g (1¾oz) fresh root ginger - 3 garlic cloves
- 90g (3¼oz) Demerara sugar - 50ml (2fl oz) oyster sauce - 100ml (3½fl oz) cooking sake
- 1 tablespoon five-spice powder - 800g (1lb 12oz) skin-on pork loin - 4 whole star anise
- Salt and freshly ground black pepper

Grater - Garlic press - Ovenproof dish

1/ Preheat the oven to 180°C fan (400°F), Gas Mark 6. Peel the pineapple, remove the core and cut the remaining flesh into pieces.

2/ Deseed the chilli pepper and finely chop the flesh. Peel the ginger and garlic cloves. Finely grate the ginger and crush the garlic using a garlic press.

3/ In a bowl, mix the garlic, sugar, ginger, chilli pepper, oyster sauce, sake and five-spice.

4/ Place the meat in an ovenproof dish and spread the pineapple around it. Pour the marinade over the meat and then season to taste.

5/ Coarsely crush the star anise and add all around the pork loin. Roast for 1½ hours, taking care to regularly baste the pork with the marinade (spoon the liquid over the surface of the meat).

EXTRA STRONG

STRONG

MEDIUM

MILD

MAPO TOFU

ϵϵϵϵ

PREPARATION: 15 MINS / COOKING: 10 MINS

SERVES 4

▪ 250g (9oz) firm tofu ▪ 2 garlic cloves ▪ 10g (¼oz) fresh root ginger ▪ 1 spring onion
▪ 2 dried chi-chien chilli peppers ▪ 2 tablespoons sunflower oil ▪ 200g (7oz) minced pork
▪ 1 tablespoon doubanjiang (fermented bean and chilli paste) ▪ 1 tablespoon douchi
(fermented black soybean paste) ▪ 2 tablespoons soy sauce ▪ 1 pinch of caster sugar
▪ 200ml (⅓ pint) chicken stock ▪ 2 teaspoons potato starch ▪ ½ teaspoon crushed
Sichuan peppercorns

Garlic press ▪ Grater ▪ Wok

1/ Cut the tofu into cubes. Bring a large saucepan of salted water to the boil. Add the tofu cubes and let them boil for 1 minute. Drain carefully and cool under cold water.

2/ Peel the garlic cloves and ginger. Crush the garlic using a garlic press and finely grate the ginger. Finely chop the spring onion. Crush the chillies.

3/ Heat the oil in a wok then add the minced pork. Brown it for 2 minutes over high heat then add the doubanjiang, douchi, soy sauce, sugar, ginger, garlic and pre-crushed chillies. Mix well.

4/ Pour in the stock and bring to the boil. Then lower the heat and add the tofu, cover and simmer for 3 minutes.

5/ Dilute the potato starch in 3 tablespoons of warm water and add it to the mixture. Increase the heat to thicken the sauce.

6/ Sprinkle over crushed Sichuan peppercorns and scatter with chopped spring onion to serve.

EXTRA STRONG | STRONG | MEDIUM | MILD

TIP
Doubanjiang and douchi can be sourced from Asian supermarkets.

CHICKEN

WITH CASHEW NUTS

𝄞 𝄞 𝄞 𝄞

PREPARATION: 30 MINS / COOKING: 15 MINS

SERVES 4

- 500g (1lb 2oz) chicken breast • 2 tablespoons soy sauce • 3 spring onions
- 3 garlic cloves • 2cm (¾ inch) piece of fresh root ginger • 1 sweet green pepper
- 1 sweet red pepper • 2 chi-chien chilli peppers • 60g (2¼oz) raw cashew nuts
- 2 tablespoons sunflower oil **FOR THE SAUCE** • 2 tablespoons black rice vinegar
- 1 tablespoon soy sauce • 1 tablespoon clear honey • 1 tablespoon Shaoxing
(Chinese cooking wine) • 1 teaspoon potato starch • 3 tablespoons water

---

Garlic press • Grater • Wok

1/ Cut the chicken into strips and marinate them in soy sauce while you prepare the rest of the ingredients.

2/ Peel the spring onions, garlic cloves and ginger. Finely chop one of the spring onions, crush the garlic cloves with a garlic press and finely grate the ginger. Remove the stems from the sweet chillies. Remove the seeds and membranes and cut the flesh into thin strips. Crush the chi-chien chilli peppers until they crumble. Chop the remaining two spring onions.

3/ Dry roast the cashew nuts for 5 minutes in a hot pan, stirring regularly so that they do not burn.

4/ **PREPARE THE SAUCE.** Mix all the sauce ingredients in the bowl.

5/ Heat the oil in a wok, add the chicken and brown it over high heat for 3 or 4 minutes. Add the one finely chopped spring onion, garlic, ginger, chi-chien chilli pepper and sweet peppers and continue cooking for 3 minutes. Pour in the sauce, mix well and continue cooking for 1 minute.

6/ Remove from the heat, add the cashew nuts, sprinkle with chopped spring onion and serve immediately.

EXTRA STRONG | STRONG | MEDIUM | MILD

SERVING SUGGESTION
Serve with Thai rice.

BIRD'S EYE CHILLI PEPPER

10

9

▶ 8

7

6

5

4

3

2

1

0

SIZE
1–2cm (½–¾ inch)

ORIGIN
This chilli pepper is from Africa.

WHERE IS IT EATEN?
It is found mainly in the Antilles,
Africa and Réunion.

EATING
It is found in lots of cuisines:
Caribbean, Asian, African,
Réunion. It is used in many
recipes, including to enhance
oils and season sauces, and
in stews or curries.

PLANT
The bird's eye chilli pepper
belongs to the nightshade
family, specifically to the species
Capsicum frutescens.

It is rated 8 on the simplified Scoville scale.

Bird's eye chilli pepper is also nicknamed
'martin's pepper' in French after the myna
bird. Previously, this chilli pepper grew in
sugarcane fields where it was eaten by birds
and the seeds were spread everywhere in their
droppings. Now, with pesticide treatments
on crops, chilli peppers no longer grow in
the fields.

Today, bird's eye chilli pepper is grown
mainly in Africa (Uganda, Madagascar,
Congo and Zanzibar).

SERVING SUGGESTION
Serve with rice.

SAUSAGE STEW

ϵϵϵϵ

PREPARATION: 15 MINS / COOKING: 35 MINS

SERVES 4

- 4 smoked pork sausages • 2 garlic cloves • 2 onions • 1 bird's eye chilli pepper
- 3 tablespoons sunflower oil • 4 thyme sprigs • 400g (14oz) can of chopped tomatoes drained of their juice • 1 bay leaf • 1 teaspoon ground turmeric
- Salt and freshly ground black pepper

Pestle and mortar • Large casserole pot

1/ Prick the sausages. Fill a large saucepan with boiling water and immerse the sausages for 10 minutes to remove the fat.

2/ Meanwhile, peel the garlic cloves and chop the onions. Remove the stem and seeds from the chilli pepper.

3/ Using a pestle and mortar, crush the garlic cloves and the chilli pepper flesh to make a paste.

4/ Heat the oil in a large casserole pot. Add the onions and chilli paste. Mix well and brown over low heat for 10 minutes.

5/ Strip the leaves from the thyme sprigs. Drain the sausages and cut them into slices 1cm (½ inch) thick. Place them in the casserole pot and brown them for 2 or 3 minutes with the chilli and onion mix. Then add the chopped tomatoes, thyme, bay leaf and turmeric. Season with salt and black pepper.

6/ Simmer for 20 minutes.

EXTRA STRONG | STRONG | MEDIUM | MILD

BIRD'S EYE CHILLI FRITTERS

ℓ ℓ ℓ ℓ

PREPARATION: 45 MINS / SOAKING: 12 HOURS / COOKING: 3–4 MINS PER BATCH

MAKES APPROXIMATELY 25 PIECES

▪ 250g (9oz) white haricot beans, dried ▪ 10 fresh coriander sprigs ▪ 4 spring onions
▪ 3cm (1¼ inch) piece of fresh root ginger ▪ 1 ripe banana ▪ 2 garlic cloves ▪ 2 small bird's
eye chilli peppers ▪ 2 teaspoons ground turmeric ▪ 2 teaspoons ground cumin
▪ 1 lime ▪ Frying oil ▪ Salt

Blender ▪ Grater ▪ Garlic press

1/ The day before you want to eat the dish, soak the beans in cold water.

2/ On the day of serving, rinse the beans under cold water. Drain them and remove the skin (optional), then blend them.

3/ Wash, dry and chop the coriander leaves and stems. Finely slice the spring onions. Peel the ginger and grate it. Mash the banana with a fork. Peel the garlic cloves and crush them using a garlic press. Remove the stems and seeds from the chilli peppers and finely chop the flesh. Mix all the ingredients with the blended beans, spices and salt. Squeeze the lime.

4/ Heat the oil to 180°C (350°F) in a sauté pan or a deep frying pan or until a small piece of bread thrown into the oil browns in 30–40 seconds. Wet your hands, take 1 tablespoonful of the mixed ingredients and form a ball. Make a small hole in the centre of each ball to help it cook through. Working in small batches, fry the balls in the oil for 3 or 4 minutes until golden brown. Remove from the oil and drain on kitchen paper.

5/ Serve hot with lime juice squeezed over.

EXTRA STRONG | STRONG | MEDIUM | MILD

CHICKEN CURRY

ℓℓℓℓ

PREPARATION: 15 MINS / COOKING: APPROXIMATELY 50 MINS

SERVES 4

- 1 whole chicken, about 1kg (2lb 4oz) - 4 tomatoes - 6 garlic cloves
- 4 onions - 2 bird's eye chilli peppers - ½ teaspoon salt - 2 thyme sprigs
- 1 teaspoon ground turmeric - 2 tablespoons sunflower oil

Pestle and mortar

1/ Cut the chicken into pieces. Remove the stems and seeds from the tomatoes, and dice them. Peel the garlic cloves and chop the onions. Remove the stems and seeds from the chilli peppers.

2/ Using a pestle and mortar, pound together the chillies, salt and garlic cloves. Strip the leaves from the thyme sprigs.

3/ Heat the oil in a heavy-based casserole pot. Add the chicken pieces and brown them on all sides for 5 minutes. Add the onions and continue cooking for 5 minutes. Add the garlic and chilli mix and brown for 3 minutes. Add the diced tomatoes, turmeric and thyme leaves, and adjust the seasoning. Pour in enough water to cover the chicken, and simmer for about 35 minutes.

4/ Serve hot.

EXTRA STRONG | STRONG | MEDIUM | MILD

SERVING SUGGESTION
Serve with rice.

VEGETABLE ACHAR (PICKLE)

ϵϵϵϵ

PREPARATION: 20 MINS / COOKING: 6 MINS

SERVES 4–6

▪ 150g (5½oz) carrots ▪ 150g (5½oz) white cabbage ▪ 50g (1¾oz) green beans
▪ 2 garlic cloves ▪ 25g (1oz) fresh root ginger ▪ 3 bird's eye chilli peppers ▪ 1 onion
▪ 150g (5½oz) courgette ▪ 2 tablespoons sunflower oil ▪ 1 teaspoon ground turmeric
▪ 3 tablespoons cider vinegar ▪ 1 teaspoon sea salt flakes

Pestle and mortar ▪ Heavy-based casserole pot

1/ Peel the carrots. Slice the white cabbage. Top and tail the green beans. Peel the garlic cloves and ginger. Remove the stem from the chilli peppers and remove the seeds and membranes. Chop the onion and cut the vegetables into thin strips or grate them. Using a pestle and mortar, crush the garlic cloves, ginger and chillies with the sea salt flakes.

2/ Heat the oil in a frying pan, add the onion, the chilli mixture and the turmeric, brown for 3 minutes, stirring regularly, then add the rest of the vegetables. Increase the heat slightly and cook for 2 or 3 minutes, stirring regularly. The vegetables should remain crisp.

3/ Remove from heat, add the vinegar, mix well and allow to cool before storing in an airtight container in a cool place. Consume within 1 week.

▶ | EXTRA STRONG | STRONG | MEDIUM | MILD

TIPS
If you do not like undercooked green beans, you can precook them for 4 minutes in boiling salted water. Achar – vegetable pickles – are eaten as condiments, in sandwiches, for example. They are usually very spicy. Adjust the amount of chilli to your personal spice tolerance level.

ROCOTO

10

SIZE
5cm (2 inches)

9

ORIGIN
This chilli pepper is from Peru.

▶ **8**

WHERE IS IT EATEN?
It is found in Latin America,
especially Peru. It can be easily
sourced in Europe in frozen form.

7

6

EATING
It is found in ceviches or dried
in the form of flakes, sprinkled
on fruits like mango or stuffed
like a sweet pepper.

5

4

PLANT
The plant measures approximately
60cm (24 inches). It is advisable
to use gloves when handling
the pepper.

3

2

The rocoto chilli pepper belongs
to the nightshade family,
specifically to the species
Capsicum chinense.

1

0

It has several names, including *rosa suchu*
and squash pepper (for its resemblance to
a squash ball).

It has a very fruity taste but is very spicy.

Rocoto chillies are rated 8 on the simplified
Scoville scale.

The rocoto turns from green to red when fully
ripe. It is also found in paste form in South
American grocery shops.

COD CEVICHE

WITH GREEN MANGO

ℓℓℓℓ

PREPARATION: 20 MINS / MARINATING: 15 MINS

SERVES 4

• 100g (3½oz) green mango (or green papaya) • ½ red onion • 2cm (¾ inch) piece of fresh root ginger • 4 limes • 400g (14oz) very fresh cod loin • Salt
FOR THE *LECHE DE TIGRE* • 1 garlic clove • 4 fresh coriander sprigs
• 2 tablespoons rocoto chilli paste

Grater • Mandolin • Garlic press

1/ Peel the green mango and grate it using a coarse grater. Slice the red onion thinly using a mandolin. Salt it a little and keep it cool (this will keep it crispy). Peel and finely grate the ginger. Squeeze the limes.

2/ Rinse the cod loin under cold running water and dry it using kitchen paper. Cut it into 2cm (¾ inch) strips along the length of the fillet and cut each strip to obtain cubes of fish approximately 2cm (¾ inch) on each side. Salt the fish to open the pores and allow the flavours to penetrate the flesh more easily. Pour the lime juice over the fish and add the grated ginger. Mix well and leave to marinate for 15 minutes in a cool place.

3/ **MEANWHILE, PREPARE THE *LECHE DE TIGRE*.** Peel the garlic clove and crush it using a garlic press. Rinse, dry, strip and finely chop the coriander. Mix the garlic, chilli paste and chopped coriander.

4/ Mix the fish, the *leche de tigre* and the grated mango. Sprinkle with sliced red onion and serve immediately.

EXTRA STRONG | STRONG | MEDIUM | MILD

TIPS

To avoid burns when handling rocoto chillies, wear disposable gloves when cooking. You can easily find frozen rocoto chillies in South American grocery shops or online. Rocoto chilli paste can be bought in a jar and will keep in the refrigerator for a very long time once opened.

ROCOTTO RELLENO

(STUFFED ROCOTO CHILLI PEPPER)

ℓℓℓℓ

PREPARATION: 20 MINS / COOKING: 35 MINS

SERVES 4

- 8 rocoto chilli peppers • 1 tablespoon caster sugar • 4 thin slices Gouda-style cheese
- 3 tablespoons salt **FOR THE STUFFING** • 2 garlic cloves • 1 red onion • 60g (2¼oz) peanuts
- 8 black olives, pitted • 4 tablespoons neutral vegetable oil • 1 teaspoon ground cumin
- 1 teaspoon dried oregano • 3 tablespoon rocoto chilli paste • ½ teaspoon freshly ground black pepper • 400g (14oz) minced meat • Salt and freshly ground black pepper

---

Disposable gloves • Ovenproof dish

1/ Slice the tops off the chilli peppers and reserve. Remove all seeds, filaments and membranes from inside each chilli pepper. Bring a large saucepan of water to the boil and add 1 tablespoon of salt. Add the chillies, wait for the mixture to boil again, cover and simmer for 3 minutes. Drain the chillies and repeat the process 2 more times, adding a tablespoonful of salt each time. For the third time, add the sugar to the water as well as the salt. Drain the chilli peppers and place them upside down on kitchen paper.

2/ **FOR THE STUFFING.** Peel the garlic cloves. Finely chop the garlic and onion. Finely chop the peanuts and crush the olives. Heat the oil in a large frying pan and add the onion and cumin and brown for 5 minutes. Add the garlic cloves, oregano, rocoto paste and black pepper. Continue cooking for 2 minutes then add the meat. Adjust the seasoning and cook for 10 minutes over high heat, stirring regularly. Add the peanuts and crushed olives.

3/ Preheat the oven to 180°C fan (400°F), Gas Mark 6. Oil an ovenproof dish. Cut the cheese slices in half. Stuff the peppers with the mixture and top each with a half slice of cheese. Replace the pepper top as a lid and place the stuffed pepper in the ovenproof dish. Bake for about 15 minutes.

EXTRA STRONG | STRONG | MEDIUM | MILD

CAYENNE CHILLI PEPPER

10

9

8 ▶

7

6

5

4

3

2

1

0

SIZE
4–5cm (1½–2 inches)

ORIGIN
This pepper is from Guyana.

WHERE IS IT EATEN?
It is found all over the world.

EATING
Cayenne chilli pepper can be used in many recipes. There is no typical recipe and it can be used in South American, Asian or American cuisines (in dishes such as chilli con carne, curry and marinated pork ribs). It can be used whole, in flakes or ground, depending on the recipe.

PLANT
Cayenne chilli pepper belongs to the nightshade family, specifically to the species *Capsicum frutescens*.

It is rated 8 on the simplified Scoville scale.

It is also known as 'devil's pepper' or '*piment enragé*' – angry pepper! The name comes from the capital of French Guiana, a city known for its infamous penal colony on Devil's Island, where the chilli peppers were grown.

Spanish conquistadors used ground cayenne chilli pepper as a substitute for black pepper and soon after, the chilli peppers became known in the major cities of Europe. In the 19th century, they were highly prized in Great Britain for seasoning dishes from the British Crown colony of India.

Cayenne chilli pepper of the *Capsicum frutescens* variety, which is hot, fruity and slightly smoky, should not be confused with cayenne pepper of the *Capsicum annuum* variety, which is a fairly ordinary mild pepper.

Cayenne chilli pepper is sometimes just referred to as 'cayenne pepper', but this is a mistake. Cayenne pepper is actually dried and ground cayenne chilli mixed with flour and salt.

SERVING SUGGESTION
Serve with white rice and black or kidney beans.

JERK CHICKEN

ℓℓℓℓ

PREPARATION: 15 MINS / MARINATING: 12 HOURS / COOKING: 45 MINS

SERVES 4

▪ 1 lime ▪ 4 tablespoons olive oil ▪ 4 tablespoons cider vinegar ▪ 2 teaspoons Demerara sugar ▪ 4 chicken thighs **FOR THE SPICE MIX** ▪ 1½ teaspoons ground nutmeg ▪ 1½ teaspoons freshly ground black pepper ▪ 1½ teaspoons ground allspice ▪ 1½ teaspoons cayenne chilli powder ▪ 2 teaspoons onion granules ▪ 1½ teaspoons garlic granules ▪ 1 teaspoon ground ginger ▪ 1 teaspoon thyme leaves ▪ 1 teaspoon ground cinnamon ▪ 1 teaspoon salt **TO SERVE** ▪ Fresh coriander

Pestle and mortar or small blender ▪ Ovenproof dish

1/ FIRST PREPARE THE SPICE MIX. Using a pestle and mortar or a small blender, blend all the spices to obtain a powder.

2/ Measure 3 tablespoons of the spice mixture into a deep dish. Squeeze the lime and add the juice to the dish, along with the olive oil, vinegar and sugar. Mix thoroughly then add the chicken thighs. Coat the chicken thighs well in the marinade. Cover and leave to marinate for 12 hours in the refrigerator.

3/ Preheat the oven to 180°C fan (400°F), Gas Mark 6. Roughly drain the chicken thighs. Place them in an ovenproof dish and bake for 45 minutes, basting them regularly with the cooking juices.

4/ Serve sprinkled with chopped coriander.

EXTRA STRONG | STRONG | MEDIUM | MILD

MONKFISH STEW

ℓℓℓℓ

PREPARATION: 15 MINS / COOKING: APPROXIMATELY 35 MINS

SERVES 4

- 1 garlic clove • 4 shallots • 1 onion • 1kg (2lb 4oz) monkfish tail, skin off • 15g (½oz) butter • 2 tablespoons olive oil • 50ml (2fl oz) cognac • 227g (8oz) can of chopped tomatoes • 2 tablespoons tomato purée • 200ml (⅓ pint) white cooking wine • ½ teaspoon cayenne pepper flakes • A few flat leaf parsley sprigs • Salt and freshly ground black pepper

Garlic press • Heavy-based casserole pot

1/ Peel the garlic and crush using a garlic press. Chop the shallots and onion.

2/ Remove the central bone and cut the monkfish into pieces.

3/ In a heavy-based casserole pot, heat the butter and oil. Brown the monkfish pieces over high heat for 2 or 3 minutes and flambé them with the cognac (add the cognac to the pan and ignite the fumes – not the liquid itself – with a long match and allow to cook until the flame goes out). Remove the fish from the casserole pot. Set aside.

4/ Add the shallots, onion, garlic, tomatoes, tomato purée, white wine, cayenne pepper, salt and pepper, and cover the pot. Simmer for 15 minutes. Add a little water if the sauce gets too dry. Return the monkfish pieces to the pan and continue cooking for another 15 minutes. Sprinkle with chopped parsley and serve immediately.

EXTRA STRONG

STRONG

MEDIUM

MILD

PORK RIBS

WITH BARBECUE SAUCE

ℓℓℓℓ

PREPARATION: 20 MINS / MARINATING: 12 HOURS / COOKING: 1 HOUR 25 MINS

SERVES 4

▪ 1.2kg (2lb 12oz) pork ribs **FOR THE MARINADE** ▪ 200g (7oz) ketchup ▪ 100g (3½oz) clear honey ▪ 4 tablespoons Worcestershire sauce ▪ 4 tablespoons white port ▪ 4 tablespoons red wine vinegar ▪ 1 teaspoon ground ginger ▪ 1 teaspoon cayenne chilli powder

---

Oven rack ▪ Baking tray

1/ The day before you want to eat the dish, cook the pork ribs for 1 hour in a large saucepan of salted boiling water. Drain and leave to cool.

2/ Meanwhile, mix all the marinade ingredients in a bowl.

3/ Place the boiled and drained pork ribs in a deep dish and pour over the marinade. Cover and place in the refrigerator for 12 hours.

4/ On the day of serving, preheat the oven to 180°C fan (400°F), Gas Mark 6. Place the ribs on a rack over a baking tray. Bake them for 20–25 minutes, turning them halfway through cooking and brushing them regularly with the marinade.

EXTRA STRONG

STRONG

MEDIUM

MILD

CORN ON THE COB

WITH CHILLI BUTTER

ϵϵϵϵ

PREPARATION: 10 MINS / COOKING: 15 MINS

SERVES 4

- 4 pre-cooked corn cobs **FOR THE CHILLI BUTTER** • 1 garlic clove • 6 fresh coriander sprigs • 1 tablespoon clear honey • ¼ teaspoon cayenne chilli powder • ½ teaspoon garam masala • 125g (4½oz) butter, at room temperature • Salt and freshly ground black pepper

---

Garlic press • Brush • Grill pan

1/ **PREPARE THE CHILLI BUTTER.** Peel the garlic clove, then crush it using a garlic press. Rinse, dry, strip and finely chop the coriander. Mix together the honey, garlic, coriander, chilli powder, garam masala and softened butter. Season.

2/ Cut each cob into 2 or 3 sections. Using a brush, cover the corn cobs with chilli butter.

3/ Brown them for 15 minutes in a grill pan, turning them regularly until they are golden.

4/ Serve hot with the remaining chilli butter.

EXTRA STRONG

STRONG

MEDIUM

MILD

THAI BIRD'S EYE CHILLI PEPPER

10

9 ▶

8

7

6

5

4

3

2

1

0

SIZE
3–4cm (1¼–1½ inches)

ORIGIN
This pepper is from Central and South America.

WHERE IS IT EATEN?
It is found in Asia and India.

EATING
This chilli pepper is found in Thai, Laotian, Cambodian, Indonesian and Vietnamese cuisines (in dishes such as Thai curry, laab moo and nasi goreng).

PLANT
Thai bird's eye chilli pepper belongs to the nightshade family, specifically to the species *Capsicum annuum*.

It is rated 9 on the simplified Scoville scale.

Thai bird's eye chilli pepper was first brought to Europe by Spanish and Portuguese explorers. These days its use is widespread in Southeast Asia but it is also cultivated in India and features heavily in Keralan cuisine.

It is also called simply bird's eye chilli or dragon chilli.

It is a small conical chilli pepper weighing no more than 3g (⅒oz). It changes from green to red as it ripens.

TIPS Serve with brown jasmine rice. Curry always tastes better the next day: if you have time, prepare the curry the day before. On the day of serving, add the prawns and cook for 10 minutes.

VARIATION You can replace the prawns with chicken. In that case, brown it for 3 or 4 minutes at the same time as the curry paste.

RED PRAWN CURRY

ℓℓℓℓ

PREPARATION: 15 MINS / COOKING: 30 MINS

SERVES 4–6

▪ 320g (11½oz) raw unpeeled prawns ▪ 2 garlic cloves ▪ 2 carrots ▪ 6 Thai aubergines ▪ 2 lemon grass stalks ▪ 2 tablespoons neutral oil ▪ 3 tablespoons Thai Red Curry Paste (see page 196) ▪ 1 litre (1¾ pints) coconut milk ▪ 6 makrut lime leaves ▪ 1 teaspoon shrimp paste ▪ 4 tablespoons fish sauce (nam pla) ▪ 2 tablespoons caster sugar ▪ 10 Thai basil leaves (plus a few for garnish)

Heavy-based casserole pot

1/ Peel the prawns and devein (remove the small black thread) using a sharp knife. Set the prawns aside.

2/ Peel the garlic cloves then crush them with the flat of a knife. Peel and slice the carrots. Wash and dry the aubergines and cut them into quarters. Remove the first leaf from the lemon grass stalks, cut the fleshy part into strips 2cm (¾ inch) thick then the rest of the sticks into 3 or 4 sections.

3/ In a heavy-based casserole pot, gently cook the garlic cloves in the oil for 2 minutes, then add the curry paste and let the flavours develop for another 2 minutes.

4/ Add the coconut milk, lemon grass, carrots, Thai aubergines, makrut lime leaves, shrimp paste, fish sauce, caster sugar and Thai basil leaves.

5/ Cook for 15 minutes over low heat, then add the prawns and continue cooking for another 10 minutes. Garnish with Thai basil leaves to serve.

EXTRA STRONG

STRONG

MEDIUM

MILD

GREEN CHICKEN CURRY

PREPARATION: 40 MINS / COOKING: 25 MINS

SERVES 4-6

FOR THE PASTE · 2 teaspoons coriander seeds · 2 teaspoons cumin seeds · 6 green Thai bird's eye chilli peppers · 1 makrut lime · 1 teaspoon whole black peppercorns · 1 teaspoon coarse salt · 2 teaspoons grated galangal · 6 tablespoons sliced lemon grass · 6 makrut lime leaves · 4 tablespoons chopped fresh coriander stems · 4 tablespoons chopped shallots · 2 tablespoons chopped garlic · 2 tablespoons shrimp paste · 2 tablespoons ground turmeric · 10 Thai basil leaves **FOR THE CURRY** · 360g (12oz) chicken breast · 2 garlic cloves · 2 tablespoons neutral oil · 2 carrots · 6 Thai aubergines · 1 lemon grass stalk · 1 litre (1¾ pints) coconut milk · 15-20 'pea' aubergines (very small aubergines, optional) · 6 makrut lime leaves · 1 tablespoon shrimp paste · 4 tablespoons fish sauce (nam pla) · 2 tablespoons brown sugar · 10 Thai basil leaves · A little makrut lime zest for garnish

Pestle and mortar or blender · Heavy-based casserole pot

1/ **PREPARE THE CURRY PASTE.** In a large frying pan, dry roast the coriander and cumin seeds. Keep a careful eye on them, to ensure the seeds do not burn. Remove the stems and seeds from the chillies. Zest the lime. Using a pestle and mortar or blender, blend all the curry paste ingredients together. Set aside.

2/ **PREPARE THE CURRY.** Cut the chicken breasts into strips. Peel the garlic cloves and crush them with the flat of a knife.

3/ In a heavy-based casserole pot, brown the garlic cloves and chicken strips in the oil for 2 minutes then add 5 tablespoons of curry paste and let the flavours develop for 2 minutes.

4/ Meanwhile, peel the carrots. Cut them into ½cm (¼ inch) slices and cut the Thai aubergines into quarters. Remove the first leaf from the lemon grass stalk, cut the fleshy part into strips 2cm (¾ inch) thick then the rest of the stick into 3 or 4 sections. Add the coconut milk, lemon grass, carrots, aubergines and pea aubergines, makrut lime leaves, shrimp paste, fish sauce and brown sugar to the casserole pot. Cook for 15 minutes.

5/ Sprinkle with Thai basil leaves and makrut lime zest and serve immediately.

TIPS Serve with white rice. Green curry paste will keep for at least 2 weeks in the refrigerator in an airtight container; you can also freeze it for longer storage.

RED CURRY FISH MOUSSE

SERVES 4

- 250g (9oz) white fish (such as cod) • 1 tablespoon Thai Red Curry Paste (see page 196)
- 2 tablespoons fish sauce (nam pla) • 1 tablespoon palm sugar or brown sugar
- 1 egg, beaten • 150ml (¼ pint) very cold coconut milk plus 4 tablespoons for garnish
- 5 makrut lime leaves • 8 Thai basil leaves • Salt and freshly ground black pepper

---

Blender • 4 ramekins • Steamer

1/ Rinse the fish under cold running water. Dry it on kitchen paper and cut it into 2cm (¾ inch) cubes. Reserve 4 cubes.

2/ In a blender, mix together the remaining fish, the curry paste, the fish sauce, the sugar and the beaten egg. Gradually pour in the coconut milk, add half of the makrut lime leaves and the Thai basil while continuing to mix. Adjust the seasoning.

3/ Place 1 cube of fish at the bottom of each ramekin. Cover with fish mousse. Over the top of each ramekin pour 1 tablespoon of coconut milk and scatter the remaining chopped makrut lime leaves over it.

4/ Steam for 15 minutes (adjust the cooking time based on the shape of the container).

5/ Serve warm or cold.

EXTRA STRONG

STRONG ▶

MEDIUM

MILD

TIP
If you have time, tom ka kai will be much tastier if you make it the day before.

TOM KA KAI

ϵϵϵϵ

PREPARATION: 15 MINS / COOKING: 15 MINS

SERVES 6

- 400g (14oz) chicken breast fillets ▪ 50g (1¾oz) piece of galangal ▪ 2 lemon grass stalks
▪ 2 green Thai bird's eye chilli peppers ▪ 3 limes ▪ 2 tablespoons neutral oil
▪ 850ml (1½ pints) coconut milk ▪ 3 bergamot leaves ▪ 200g (7oz) mushrooms
▪ 2 tablespoons fish sauce (nam pla) ▪ 1 teaspoon caster sugar ▪ ¼ teaspoon salt

1/ Cut the chicken fillets into small pieces and set aside.

2/ Peel the galangal and cut it into 1cm (½ inch) pieces. Set aside.

3/ Remove the first leaf from the lemon grass stalks, cut them diagonally into 3cm (1¼ inch) pieces. Set aside.

4/ Remove the stalks and seeds from the chillies and chop the flesh finely. Squeeze the limes.

5/ Brown the chicken pieces for 5 minutes in the oil in a casserole pot, stirring regularly. Add the coconut milk, bergamot leaves, chilli peppers, mushrooms, fish sauce, lime juice and sugar. Add salt to taste. Simmer for 10 minutes over low heat (do not allow the mixture to boil).

EXTRA STRONG |

▶ STRONG |

MEDIUM |

MILD |

BABY SQUID SALAD

WITH CUCUMBER AND SESAME OIL

ℓ ℓ ℓ ℓ

PREPARATION: 15 MINS / COOKING: 2 MINS

SERVES 4

▪ 500g (1lb 2oz) prepared baby squid ▪ 2 mini cucumbers ▪ 8 cherry tomatoes
▪ 1 garlic clove ▪ 1 shallot ▪ 2 tablespoons peanuts ▪ 1 or 2 red Thai bird's eye chilli
peppers (depending on your chilli tolerance level) ▪ A few fresh coriander sprigs
▪ 4 tablespoons rice vinegar ▪ 1 teaspoon caster sugar ▪ 2 tablespoons sesame oil
▪ 4 tablespoons fish sauce (nam pla)

Garlic press

1/ Cook the baby squid for 2 minutes in simmering water. Drain them and leave to cool.

2/ Wash and dry the cucumbers and cherry tomatoes. Cut the cucumber into slices and the cherry tomatoes into quarters.

3/ Peel the garlic clove and the shallot. Chop the shallot and crush the garlic clove with a garlic press.

4/ Toast the peanuts in a hot, dry pan and chop them coarsely.

5/ Remove the stalk and seeds from the chilli pepper and chop the flesh finely.

6/ Wash, dry and strip the coriander leaves, then chop.

7/ Mix the shallot, garlic, rice vinegar, sugar, chilli pepper, sesame oil and fish sauce in a large bowl. Add the baby squid, mix and refrigerate until ready to serve.

EXTRA STRONG | STRONG | MEDIUM | MILD

TIPS Serve with white rice or sticky rice. Adjust the amount of chilli depending on your taste and spice tolerance.

VARIATIONS If you cannot find Thai green beans, you can use regular green beans. Similarly, you can replace the palm sugar with 2 tablespoons caster sugar. Try the same recipe with green mango.

GREEN PAPAYA

SALAD

ℓℓℓℓ

PREPARATION: 15 MINS / COOKING: 5 MINS

SERVES 4

• 1 green papaya, about 400g (14oz) • 12 cherry tomatoes • 100g (3½oz) raw
Thai green beans • 1 lime • 1 garlic clove • 40g (1½oz) raw unsalted peanuts
• 1 small piece of palm sugar • 1 red Thai bird's eye chilli pepper • 1 green Thai bird's
eye chilli pepper • 4 tablespoons fish sauce (nam pla) • 4 tablespoons dried shrimp
(from the frozen section of Asian grocery shops) • Salt
TO SERVE • 4 portions cooked ribbon noodles (optional)

Coarse grater or vegetable peeler • Pestle and mortar

---

1 / Rinse the fruit and vegetables. Peel the papaya then grate it using a coarse grater or
a vegetable peeler (this is ideal for cutting the papaya into long, thin strips). Cut the
cherry tomatoes into quarters, cut the green beans into 1cm (½ inch) pieces. Squeeze
the lime. Peel the garlic clove.

2 / In a hot pan, toast the peanuts for 5 minutes then crush them coarsely. Set aside.

3 / Using a pestle and mortar, combine the papaya, cherry tomatoes, beans, lime juice and
garlic. Add the palm sugar, chilli peppers, fish sauce and dried shrimp. Season to taste.
Mix well with a spoon then use the pestle to extract the juice from all the vegetables.
Transfer the salad to a large bowl and stir through the cooked noodles, if using.

4 / Divide the papaya salad between the serving plates and sprinkle with crushed peanuts.

EXTRA STRONG | STRONG | MEDIUM | MILD

SERVING SUGGESTION
Serve with sticky rice or Thai rice.

PORK LAAB

MOO

ℓℓℓℓ

PREPARATION: 20 MINS / COOKING: 5 MINS

SERVES 4

- 15g (½oz) rice, preferably sticky - 30g (1oz) piece of galangal
- 1 lemon grass stalk - 2 limes - 2 red Thai bird's eye chilli peppers - 1 red onion
- leaves from 8 mint sprigs - 400g (14oz) minced pork - 2 tablespoons neutral oil
- 4 tablespoons fish sauce (nam pla) - Salt and freshly ground black pepper

---

Pestle and mortar - Blender

1/ In a dry frying pan, toast the rice. Once the grains are golden, crush them coarsely using a pestle and mortar.

2/ Peel the galangal. Remove the first leaf from the lemon grass stalk and finely slice the fleshiest part of the stem. Squeeze the limes.

3/ Remove the stalks and seeds from the chillies and chop the flesh finely.

4/ Using a blender, chop together the onion, galangal and mint leaves.

5/ Over high heat, brown the minced pork for a few minutes in the oil. Mix it with all the condiments, chopped chillies and toasted rice. Adjust the seasoning.

EXTRA STRONG

STRONG

MEDIUM

MILD

HABANERO

10

—

SIZE
5cm (2 inches)

9

—

ORIGIN
This pepper is native to Mexico.

8

—

WHERE IS IT EATEN?
It is found in the Antilles but also in Africa and Réunion.

7

—

EATING
In the Antilles, it is found in cod chiktail, cod fritters, colombo and spicy avocado dip. In Réunion, it is used to make chilli paste. It is part of the traditional Malagasy dish *vary sy laoka*.

6

—

5

—

4

—

PLANT
The habanero chilli pepper belongs to the nightshade family, specifically to the species *Capsicum chinense*.

3

—

2

—

1

—

0

—

This is a very hot chilli pepper. It is rated 9–10 on the simplified Scoville scale.

In the Antilles, it is called bondamanjak pepper or goat pepper in Réunion.

It is round and swollen, green, yellow, orange or red, depending on its ripeness. It has a lemony flavour and floral aromas. Due to the heat of this chilli, it is best to use gloves when handling it.

The habanero chilli is not eaten on its own. It is simmered in dishes during cooking to flavour them and removed before serving, or the food can be rubbed with chilli beforehand. It can also be used to flavour alcohol.

It can be found fresh, in brine or as a paste.

Until 2006, it was the hottest chilli pepper recorded (see page 6).

CHICKEN ACCRAS (FRITTERS)

ℓℓℓℓ

PREPARATION: 25 MINS / COOKING: 3–4 MINS PER BATCH

SERVES 4–6 (APPROXIMATELY 25 PIECES)

• 300g (10½oz) leftover roast chicken • 4 flat leaf parsley sprigs • 2 garlic cloves
• 1 red onion • 2 limes • 300g (10½oz) plain flour • 1 habanero chilli pepper
• 1 teaspoon bicarbonate of soda • Frying oil • Salt and freshly ground black pepper

---

Pestle and mortar

1/ Shred the roast chicken. Wash, dry, strip and chop the parsley leaves. Peel the garlic cloves. Finely chop the garlic and onion. Squeeze one of the limes.

2/ In a bowl, mix the shredded chicken, garlic, onion and parsley well.

3/ Place the flour in another bowl, make a well in the centre and pour in 250ml (9fl oz) of water. Mix well.

4/ Roughly crush the chilli pepper in 100ml (3½fl oz) of water then take it out. Add the bicarbonate of soda and lime juice. Pour this mixture over the batter, mix well and add the chicken mixture.

5/ Heat the frying oil in a sauté pan or a deep frying pan to 180°C (350°F), or until a small piece of bread thrown into the oil browns in 30–40 seconds. You need enough oil to cover the accras. Using a spoon, make small mounds of batter and fry them for 3 or 4 minutes, turning them regularly. Fry in small batches.

6/ Drain the accras on kitchen paper and serve hot with the remaining lime cut into wedges on the side.

EXTRA STRONG | STRONG | MEDIUM | MILD

SPICY AVOCADO AND SALT COD DIP

ℓℓℓℓ

PREPARATION: 25 MINS / COOKING: 30 MINS

SERVES 4

▪ 1 habanero chilli pepper ▪ 200g (7oz) salt cod ▪ 2 garlic cloves ▪ 2 spring onions or ½ white onion ▪ 2 flat leaf parsley sprigs ▪ 1 lime ▪ 2 avocados ▪ 50g (1¾oz) cassava flour ▪ 4 tablespoons olive or rapeseed oil ▪ Salt and freshly ground black pepper

---

Pestle and mortar ▪ Garlic press

1/ Crush the chilli pepper. Rinse the cod under cold running water to remove all the salt. Place it in a pan of cold water, bring to the boil then simmer for 10 minutes. Drain. Repeat the process 3 times, carefully adding the crushed chilli pepper to the last cooking water. Drain the cod and flake it.

2/ Peel the garlic cloves and crush them using a garlic press. Finely chop the onions. Wash, dry, strip and chop the parsley. Squeeze the lime.

3/ Cut the avocados in half and remove the stones. Mash the flesh with a fork, add the lime juice, crushed garlic and chopped onion. Add the cassava flour and oil, and mix well until you get a spreadable texture. Stir through the flaked cod until mixed well. Adjust the seasoning.

4/ Keep cool – but not for too long as the avocado will discolour – until serving.

EXTRA STRONG | STRONG | MEDIUM ▶ | MILD

OTHER SPICY FLAVOURS

There are other hot flavours besides chilli, including mustard, ginger and wasabi. In these flavours, the spiciness is not from the capsaicin molecule.

Gingerol gives ginger its spiciness. It is strongest when the ginger is fresh, and less so when the ginger is dry or cooked.

For mustard, the spiciness comes from the molecules sinigrin and myrosin. When they are crushed, a chemical reaction transforms them into organosulfur molecules, which stimulate the trigeminal nerve in the mouth, creating a very strong and potentially unpleasant sensation.

Wasabi root is rich in isothiocyanates and sinigrin. When these molecules are crushed, an enzymatic reaction is triggered which stimulates the trigeminal nerve in a similar way to mustard.

TIP
Adjust the cooking time depending on how rare you want the meat.

BEEF FILLET

WITH A HERB AND MUSTARD CRUST

PREPARATION: 15 MINS / COOKING: 25 MINS

SERVES 4–6

- 6 flat leaf parsley sprigs - 6 mint sprigs - 6 chervil sprigs - 1 garlic clove
- 40g (1½oz) butter, at room temperature - 40g (1½oz) breadcrumbs - 3 tablespoons
strong mustard - 800g (1lb 12oz) beef (tenderloin or a middle cut fillet)
- Salt and freshly ground black pepper

Ovenproof dish

1/ Wash, dry and strip the herbs. Peel the garlic clove.

2/ Chop the herbs with the garlic clove. Add the softened butter, breadcrumbs and mustard, and mix until you have a paste. Season with salt and black pepper.

3/ Preheat the oven to 240°C fan (500°F), Gas Mark 10, or the hottest setting available. Cover the top of the beef with the paste, place it in an ovenproof dish and roast for 25 minutes (for rare meat).

EXTRA STRONG

STRONG

MEDIUM

MILD

TOMATO AND MUSTARD
TART

ϵϵϵϵ

PREPARATION: 15 MINS / COOKING: 30 MINS

SERVES 4

- 1 sheet of ready-rolled puff pastry, about 320g (11½oz) • 4 tomatoes • 8 yellow cherry tomatoes • 3 tablespoons wholegrain mustard • 3 tablespoons strong mustard • 2 thyme sprigs • 1 tablespoon clear honey • 1 egg, beaten (for glazing)

Baking tray • Nonstick baking paper

1/ Preheat the oven to 200°C fan (425°F), Gas Mark 7. Spread the pastry on a baking tray lined with nonstick baking paper.

2/ Wash and dry the tomatoes and cherry tomatoes. Remove the stems and cut them into thin slices.

3/ Mix the wholegrain mustard and the strong mustard then spread over the sheet of pastry, taking care to leave a ½cm (¼ inch) margin around the edge.

4/ Strip the leaves from the thyme sprigs. Lay the tomatoes over the pastry. Season with salt and pepper and drizzle with honey. Sprinkle with a few thyme leaves.

5/ Brush beaten egg around the edge of the tart.

6/ Bake for 30 minutes. The tart should be golden brown.

EXTRA STRONG

STRONG

MEDIUM

▶ MILD

WASABI GRAPEFRUIT

GRANITA

ℓℓℓℓ

PREPARATION: 10 MINS / FREEZING: 12 HOURS

SERVES 4

• 500ml (18fl oz) fresh grapefruit juice • 4 tablespoons lemon juice
• 1 teaspoon wasabi paste from a tube

Blender • Freezerproof container

1/ Using a blender, mix the grapefruit juice, lemon juice and wasabi paste.

2/ Pour the mixture into a container and place it in the freezer for 12 hours.

3/ Regularly scrape the mixture with a fork until you obtain a granita texture (coarse crystals).

4/ Pour the granita into small bowls and serve immediately.

EXTRA STRONG

STRONG

MEDIUM

▶ MILD

TIP
If your tin is high-sided, extend the cooking time a little.

CHOCO-WASABI

CAKE

ᕦᕦᕦᕦ

PREPARATION: 15 MINS / COOKING: 22 MINS

SERVES 4–6

▪ 200g (7oz) dark chocolate ▪ 200g (7oz) butter (plus a little for greasing the tin)
▪ 100g (3½oz) caster sugar ▪ 5 eggs ▪ 1 tablespoon plain flour
▪ 1 teaspoon wasabi powder or paste from a tube

16cm (6¼ inch) or 20cm (8 inch) cake tin ▪ Nonstick baking paper

---

1/ Grease and line either a 16cm (6¼ inch) cake tin (for a gooey centre) or a 20cm (8 inch) cake tin (for moist cake).

2/ Preheat the oven to 190°C fan (410°C), Gas Mark 6½. Cut the butter and chocolate into small pieces and melt them in a bain-marie. (Heat a small saucepan of water. Place the bowl over the pan so that the bottom of the bowl does not touch the water.) Let it cool for a few moments and add the sugar. Mix well.

3/ Add the eggs one by one, mixing between each one. Stir through the flour and wasabi powder or paste.

4/ Pour the batter into the prepared tin and bake for 22 minutes.

EXTRA STRONG

STRONG

MEDIUM

▶ MILD

TIP
You can prepare the blinis the day before. Once cooled, wrap them in an airtight plastic bag and store them at room temperature.

CHESTNUT FLOUR BLINIS

WITH SALMON AND WASABI WHIPPED CREAM

ℓℓℓℓ

PREPARATION: 15 MINS / RESTING: 30 MINS
COOKING: 2–3 MINS PER BATCH OF BLINIS

MAKES 20 MINI-BLINIS

FOR THE BLINIS · 300ml (½ pint) milk · 70g (2½oz) wholemeal plain flour
· 70g (2½oz) chestnut flour · 1 × 7g sachet of fast-action dried yeast · 2 egg whites
· 2 pinches of fine salt · 15g (½oz) butter (for cooking the blinis)
FOR THE TOPPING · 200ml (⅓ pint) very cold double cream · 1 teaspoon wasabi paste
from a tube (or 2 tablespoons grated fresh wasabi root) · 200g (7oz) smoked salmon
· A few sesame seeds · Salt

1/ **FIRST PREPARE THE BLINIS.** Warm the milk in a saucepan. Sift the 2 flours together
with the yeast. Pour the warm milk over the flour and mix well to form a batter.
Let it rest for 30 minutes at room temperature.

2/ Beat the egg whites with the salt until stiff. Fold the egg whites into the batter using
a spatula, lifting the batter so as not to break up the egg whites.

3/ In a small frying pan, melt a little butter, add a small ladleful of batter, and cook the
blini for about 2 minutes, turning it over halfway through cooking. Repeat with the
rest of the batter, cooking 3–4 blinis at a time.

4/ **MEANWHILE, PREPARE THE TOPPING.** Mix the cream with the wasabi. Add salt to
taste. Whip the cream until stiff peaks form. Divide the salmon among the blinis
and top each with a little wasabi whipped cream. Sprinkle with sesame seeds.
Serve immediately.

| EXTRA STRONG |

| STRONG |

▶ | MEDIUM |

| MILD |

SERVING SUGGESTION
Serve with Japanese rice.

TERIYAKI SALMON

𝒸𝒸𝒸𝒸

PREPARATION: 15 MINS / MARINATING: 2 HOURS / COOKING: 24 MINS

SERVES 4

• 50g (1¾oz) piece of fresh root ginger • 4 tablespoons soy sauce • 4 tablespoons mirin
• 30g (1oz) cane sugar • 600g (1lb 5oz) salmon fillet without skin • Sesame seeds

Grater • Baking tray • Nonstick baking paper

1/ Peel the ginger and grate it.

2/ In a saucepan, mix all the marinade ingredients: soy sauce, mirin, cane sugar and grated ginger. Bring to the boil for 3 or 4 minutes. Leave to cool.

3/ Place the salmon fillets in a deep dish and pour the marinade over them.

4/ Cover and refrigerate for 2 hours.

5/ Preheat the oven to 200°C fan (425°F), Gas Mark 7. Drain the salmon fillets and arrange on a baking tray lined with nonstick baking paper. Bake for 20 minutes. After 10 minutes, brush the salmon fillets with the remaining marinade and continue cooking for another 10 minutes. Sprinkle with sesame seeds. Serve hot or cold.

EXTRA STRONG

STRONG

MEDIUM

▶ MILD

GINGER CAKE

ℓℓℓℓ

SERVES 4–6

• 100g (3½oz) fresh root ginger • 125g (4½oz) sugar cane molasses • 250ml (9fl oz) sunflower or grapeseed oil • 30g (1oz) caster sugar • 130g (4½oz) clear honey • 180ml (6fl oz) water • 2 teaspoons bicarbonate of soda • 1 teaspoon ground cinnamon, plus extra to decorate • 2 teaspoons mixed spice • 280g (10oz) plain flour • 2 eggs, beaten **FOR THE ICING** • 225g (8oz) soft cheese (Philadelphia® style) • 30g (1oz) icing sugar

Loaf tin • Nonstick baking paper • Grater • Aluminium foil

1/ Grease and line a 22 × 10cm (8½ × 4 inch) loaf tin.

2/ Preheat the oven to 180°C fan (400°F), Gas Mark 6. Peel and finely grate the ginger.

3/ In a large bowl mix the molasses, oil, sugar and honey.

4/ Bring the measured water to the boil in a saucepan. Remove from the heat, add the bicarbonate of soda and pour over the molasses mixture. Stir well. Add the ginger, spices and eggs, and mix together well then add the flour. Stir well to obtain a smooth batter.

5/ Pour the batter into the prepared tin and bake for 45 minutes. After 30 minutes, cover with aluminium foil if the cake is getting too brown on top.

6/ Remove from the oven and let the cake cool in the tin.

7/ **PREPARE THE ICING.** Mix the soft cheese with the icing sugar. Spread the mixture over the top of the cake then sprinkle with a little cinnamon to decorate.

8/ Refrigerate the cake for 2 hours before serving.

EXTRA STRONG | STRONG | MEDIUM | MILD ▶

CREAM OF CARROT SOUP

WITH SWEET POTATO, GINGER AND ORANGE

⏳⏳⏳⏳

PREPARATION: 25 MINS / COOKING: 40 MINS

SERVES 6–8

- 1kg (2lb 4oz) carrots · 500g (1lb 2oz) sweet potatoes
- 4cm (1½ inch) piece of fresh root ginger · 2 garlic cloves · 2 onions · 3 unwaxed oranges
- 4 tablespoons olive oil · 1 litre (1¾ pints) vegetable stock · 200ml (⅓ pint) coconut milk ·
A few fresh coriander sprigs · 2 tablespoons coarsely crushed unsalted pistachios
- Salt and freshly ground black pepper

Blender · Grater

1/ Wash then peel the carrots and sweet potatoes. Cut them into 1.5cm (⅝ inch) pieces. Peel and finely grate the ginger. Peel the garlic. Chop the garlic and onions. Wash the oranges, remove the zest from 2 of them and then squeeze all 3 of them.

2/ Add the olive oil to a large saucepan along with the garlic, onions and ginger. Stir well and brown for 5 minutes over medium heat. Add the carrots, orange zest (keep some back for garnishing), orange juice and stock. Cover. After 10 minutes, add the sweet potatoes and cook over a low heat for 25 minutes (the tip of a knife should easily go into the vegetables). Remove from the heat and leave to cool a little.

3/ Blend the contents of the saucepan, adding a little water if necessary to reach your desired consistency.

4/ At the last moment, pour in the coconut milk to bind everything together. Adjust the seasoning. Garnish with chopped coriander, some finely sliced orange zest and a sprinkle of coarsely crushed pistachios.

5/ Serve hot.

SUBSTITUTION
You can replace the coconut milk with double cream in the same proportions.

EXTRA STRONG | STRONG | MEDIUM | MILD

GINGER, LEMON AND MINT

INFUSION

ƹƹƹƹ

SERVES 4

- 1 unwaxed lemon ▪ 4 mint sprigs ▪ 4cm (1½ inch) piece of fresh root ginger
▪ 1 litre (1¾ pints) water

1/ Wash the lemon and mint. Cut the lemon into slices and strip the mint leaves. Peel the ginger and cut it into thin slices or grate it.

2/ Heat the water to around 85°C (185°F) and add all of the ingredients. Let them infuse for 15 minutes.

3/ Enjoy hot, warm or iced.

| EXTRA STRONG |

| STRONG |

| MEDIUM |

| MILD |

RAITA

SERVES 4

• 1 lime • 300g (10½oz) Greek yogurt • ½ ripe mango • 2cm (¾ inch) piece of fresh root ginger • 4 fresh coriander sprigs • 1½ red onions • Salt

Grater

1/ Squeeze the lime. Mix the yogurt, a pinch of salt and lime juice in a bowl.

2/ Peel the mango and cut it into small cubes. Peel the ginger and grate it with a fine grater. Wash, dry, strip and chop the coriander. Finely chop the onion.

3/ Mix all the ingredients and refrigerate. Consume within 3 days.

| EXTRA STRONG |

| STRONG |

▶ | MEDIUM |

| MILD |

SAUCES

CHIMICHURRI SAUCE

ϹϹϹϹ

PREPARATION: 15 MINS

SERVES 4

▪ 4 spring onions with green stems ▪ 2 small garlic cloves
▪ 1 small bunch of fresh coriander ▪ 2 tablespoons lemon juice ▪ 2 tablespoons
dried oregano ▪ 2 teaspoons green chilli paste ▪ 6 tablespoons olive oil

---

Blender

1/ Remove half the green stems from the spring onions. Peel the garlic cloves. Wash, dry and strip the coriander leaves.

2/ Using a blender, mix all the sauce ingredients together. Add a little more oil if the mixture seems too thick.

3/ Transfer to an airtight, sterilized jar for storage. This sauce will keep for at least 2 weeks.

EXTRA STRONG

◀

STRONG

MEDIUM

MILD

TIPS
Chimichurri sauce is delicious with meat, for example. Serve it with lime wedges.

SALSA CRIOLLA

ɾɾɾɾ

PREPARATION: 15 MINS

MAKES I JAR OF APPROXIMATELY IOOG (3½ OZ)

• ½ green sweet pepper • ½ yellow sweet pepper • ½ red sweet pepper
• ½ orange sweet pepper • 1 ají amarillo chilli pepper • 6 fresh coriander sprigs
• 3 spring onions with 2cm (¾ inch) of green stems • 1 shallot • 2 tablespoons
sunflower oil • 2 teaspoons sherry vinegar • Salt and freshly ground black pepper

---

Sterilized jar

1/ Remove the stems from the sweet peppers and the ají amarillo chilli pepper. Remove the seeds and membranes. Wash, dry, strip and chop the coriander.

2/ Finely dice the peppers, spring onions, shallot and chilli pepper. Mix them in the jar with the coriander. Pour in the oil and vinegar. Season with salt and pepper.

3/ Transfer to an airtight, sterilized jar for storage.

| EXTRA STRONG |

▶ | STRONG |

| MEDIUM |

| MILD |

|

TIP
The sauce can be stored for 2 weeks in a cool place in an airtight container.

HARISSA SALSA

ϵϵϵϵ

PREPARATION: 15 MINS / COOKING: 15 MINS

MAKES 1 JAR OF APPROXIMATELY 400G (14OZ)

▪ 50g (1¾oz) Thai bird's eye chilli peppers (about 40) ▪ 100g (3½oz) semi-dried tomatoes
▪ 50g (1¾oz) garlic (about 6 large cloves) ▪ 200ml (⅓ pint) olive oil ▪ ½ teaspoon
ground caraway ▪ 1 teaspoon chopped fresh coriander ▪ ½ teaspoon salt

---

Casserole pot ▪ Disposable gloves ▪ Blender ▪ Sterilized jar

1/ Remove the stalks and seeds from the chilli peppers and chop them. Slice the semi-dried tomatoes.

2/ Peel the garlic cloves. Pour the olive oil into a casserole pot. Add the garlic cloves and let them caramelize for 10 minutes over high heat. Then reduce the heat and add the chillies, tomatoes, spices and salt. Continue cooking for 5 minutes.

3/ Using a blender, reduce everything to a purée.

4/ Leave to cool then transfer to an airtight, sterilized jar for storage.

EXTRA STRONG | STRONG | MEDIUM | MILD

TIPS

The sauce can be stored for 2 weeks in a cool place in an airtight container. Wear gloves when cooking with Thai bird's eye chilli peppers.

SRIRACHA SAUCE

ℓℓℓℓ

PREPARATION: 15 MINS / COOKING: 20 MINS

MAKES 1 JAR OF APPROXIMATELY 300G (10½ OZ)

▪ 150g (5½oz) red jalapeño peppers ▪ 60g (2¼oz) garlic cloves (about 7 large cloves)
▪ 6 tablespoons rice vinegar ▪ 5 teaspoons agave syrup ▪ 1 tablespoon coarse salt
▪ ⅓ tablespoon cornflour ▪ 1 tablespoon fish sauce (nam pla)

Hand blender (or blender) ▪ Sterilized jar

1/ Remove the stalks, seeds and membranes from the chilli peppers and then thinly slice the flesh.

2/ Peel the garlic cloves. Place them in a small pan of water and bring to the boil. Drain then cool them under cold water and repeat the process.

3/ Put the garlic cloves, the chopped chillies and the vinegar in a medium saucepan and bring to the boil. Reduce the heat and simmer for 3 minutes. Add the agave syrup and salt, mix well and set aside to cool.

4/ Dilute the cornflour in 1 tablespoon of hot water.

5/ Using a hand blender, blend the contents of the saucepan. Add the cornflour mixture. Return to the heat and simmer for 15 minutes over low heat.

6/ Off the heat, pour in the fish sauce and mix.

7/ Leave to cool then transfer to an airtight, sterilized jar for storage.

| EXTRA STRONG |

| STRONG |

▶ | MEDIUM |

| MILD |

TIPS
The sauce can be stored for 1 week in a cool place in an airtight container.

BARBECUE SAUCE

PREPARATION: 2 MINS / COOKING: 15–20 MINS

MAKES 1 JAR OF APPROXIMATELY 400G (14OZ)

- 2 tablespoons white vinegar - 500g (1lb 2oz) ketchup - 1½ tablespoons mustard
- 2 tablespoons soy sauce - 8 tablespoons brown sugar - 200ml (⅓ pint) cola
- 6 tablespoons olive oil - 1 tablespoon chipotle chilli powder

---

Casserole pot - Sterilized jar

1/ Pour the vinegar into a small casserole pot. When it starts to boil, add the ketchup, mustard, soy sauce, sugar, cola, olive oil and chilli powder. Mix well.

2/ Let the sauce reduce by about half, stirring regularly over low heat.

3/ Leave to cool then transfer to an airtight, sterilized jar for storage.

EXTRA STRONG

STRONG

MEDIUM

MILD

TIP
The sauce can be kept for 15 days in a cool place in an airtight container.

SAMBAL OELEK SAUCE

ƐƐƐƐ

PREPARATION: 10 MINS

MAKES 1 JAR OF 100G (3½ OZ)

- 100g (3½oz) Thai bird's eye chilli peppers - ½ teaspoon salt
- 4 tablespoons vinegar of your choice

Disposable gloves - Blender - Sterilized jar

1/ Remove the stalks from the chilli peppers. Leave more or less seeds depending on how hot you want the sauce to be (the more seeds you leave, the spicier the sauce will be).

2/ Blend the chilli peppers with the salt and vinegar.

3/ Transfer to an airtight, sterilized jar for storage.

EXTRA STRONG

▶

STRONG

MEDIUM

MILD

TIPS
The sauce can be kept for 15 days in the refrigerator. Wear gloves when handling the chilli peppers, otherwise you risk burning your hands.

THAI RED CURRY PASTE

PREPARATION: 20 MINS

ʅ ʅ ʅ ʅ

MAKES 1 JAR OF APPROXIMATELY 50G (1¾OZ)

▪ 2 teaspoons coriander seeds ▪ 2 teaspoons cumin seeds ▪ 6 garlic cloves
▪ 4 small shallots ▪ 4 lemon grass stalks ▪ 6 makrut lime leaves ▪ 10 Thai basil leaves
▪ 8 red Thai bird's eye chilli peppers ▪ 1 makrut lime ▪ 1 teaspoon ground cardamom
▪ 1 teaspoon black peppercorns (whole) ▪ 1 teaspoon coarse salt ▪ 2 teaspoons grated
galangal ▪ 2 tablespoons shrimp paste ▪ 4 tablespoons chopped fresh coriander stems

---

Disposable gloves ▪ Grater ▪ Pestle and mortar (or a blender) ▪ Sterilized jar

---

1/ In a large dry frying pan, toast the coriander seeds and cumin seeds (without letting them burn).

2/ Peel the garlic cloves. Finely chop the garlic and shallots. Remove the tough ends of the lemon grass stalks, remove the first leaf and cut the stalks into quarters lengthways. Chop the makrut lime and basil leaves. Wearing gloves, remove the stems and seeds from the chillies and chop the flesh finely. Zest the lime with the grater.

3/ Using a pestle and mortar (or a blender), crush the ingredients gradually, starting with the dry ingredients: coriander seeds, cumin seeds, lemon grass, cardamom, peppercorns, salt. Then add the wet ingredients: garlic, shallots, chillies, galangal, shrimp paste, lime zest, leaves (makrut lime and basil) and coriander stems.

4/ When your paste is smooth, transfer it to an airtight sterilized jar.

EXTRA STRONG

STRONG

MEDIUM

MILD

TIP
The curry paste can be kept for 2 weeks in the refrigerator and 2 months in the freezer.

RECIPE INDEX

B

C

K

L

M

O

P

R

S

T

V

W

UK/US TERMS

UK	US
aubergine	eggplant
avocado stone	avocado pit
baking tray	baking sheet
bulgur wheat	cracked wheat
buttermilk	cultured buttermilk
cake tin	cake pan
casserole pot	Dutch oven
caster sugar	superfine sugar
coriander (fresh)	cilantro
cornflour	corn starch
courgette	zucchini
frying pan	skillet
grate	shred
grill	broil/broiler
haricot bean	navy bean
icing sugar	confectioners' sugar
kitchen paper	paper towel
loaf tin	loaf pan
minced meat/lamb	ground meat/lamb
natural yogurt	plain/unflavoured yogurt
pak choi	bok choy
plain flour	all-purpose flour
prawn	shrimp
rapeseed oil	canola oil
spring onion	scallion/green onion
tomato purée	tomato paste
sweet pepper	bell pepper

ACKNOWLEDGEMENTS

THE AUTHOR AND STYLIST

My thanks to Emanuela for her delicate light
and her investment in this work.

Thanks also to Ayumi for her advice on Japanese chillies
and to Alexanne for her help in the kitchen.

I would like to thank the entire Hachette team, and in
particular Céline Le Lamer and Séverine Corson-Schneider,
for trusting me with this wonderful project.

I dedicate this book to my son Achille and my little
celestial bumblebee.

THE PHOTOGRAPHER

What a pleasure to share this first book together, Sophie!
Thank you for your enthusiasm and the love you put into
every recipe, every detail, even the most subtle...
Thank you for your creativity, which is so enriching.

And of course, thank you both, Céline and Séverine,
for this lovely project.

First published in Great Britain in 2026 by Mitchell Beazley,
an imprint of Octopus Publishing Group Ltd,
Carmelite House, 50 Victoria Embankment,
London EC4Y 0DZ
www.octopusbooks.co.uk

An Hachette UK Company
www.hachette.co.uk

The authorized representative in the EEA is Hachette Ireland,
8 Castlecourt Centre, Dublin 15, D15 XTP3, Ireland (email: info@hbgi.ie)

Originally published as *Piments* in France by Hachette Pratique in 2025

Piments copyright © Hachette Livre (Hachette Pratique) 2025
Translation copyright © Octopus Publishing Group Ltd 2026

Distributed in the US by Hachette Book Group, 1290 Avenue of the Americas,
4th and 5th Floors, New York, NY 10104

Distributed in Canada by Canadian Manda Group, 664 Annette St,
Toronto, Ontario, Canada M6S 2C8

ISBN 978-1-84601-673-8
eISBN 978-1-84601-674-5

A CIP catalogue record for this book is available from the British Library.

Printed and bound in China.

1 3 5 7 9 10 8 6 4 2

English edition 2026
Commissioning Editor: Jeannie Stanley
Art Director: Yasia Williams
Senior Editor: Leanne Bryan
Translation from the French: Margaret Morrison
Copyeditor: Elizabeth Fletcher
Designer: Jeremy Tilston www.theoakstudio.co.uk
Production Manager: Caroline Alberti

French edition 2025
Direction: Catherine Saunier-Talec
Editorial Manager: Lisa Grall
Project Managers: Jeanne Mauboussin and Chléa Caroux
Artistic Director: Nicolas Gallois
Photographs: Emanuela Cino (except p.197 © adomer/istockphoto)
Cover illustration: Kim Roselier
Layout: Cécile Rabataud